ZEPHYR BOOKS

A Library of British and American Authors

VOL. 100

TWELVE
MODERN POETS

TWELVE
MODERN POETS

An Anthology Edited by
Artur Lundkvist

ZEPHYR
BOOKS

The Continental Book Company AB
STOCKHOLM / LONDON

INTRODUCTION

This anthology contains a representative selection of the best English poetry published during and between the two wars. Three of the twelve poets chosen were already famous in the twenties: T. S. Eliot, Ezra Pound, and Edith Sitwell; the other nine belong to a younger generation and the period since 1930. Pound is an American, but must be included as a pioneer member of the modern movement, which learnt a great deal from his masterly handling of free measures. Eliot is only an American by birth. Unlike Pound, he has fully assimilated, and been fully assimilated by, the English tradition, and since 1927 has been a British subject.

Eliot's pre-eminence is generally recognized and he has certainly contributed more than any other writer to the development of modern English poetry. With a profound sense of the past he unites an equally profound sense of his own time and dexterous contemporaneity of manner. His own development has been towards ever greater precision: he writes a concrete, objective verse as meticulous as it is complex, with studied juxtaposition of dissimilars. An undercurrent of deep *malaise* flows through all his work, from *Prufrock* in 1917 to *Four Quartets* in 1945, charging it with a keen and distinctive poignancy.

Pound has always been the experimenter, fond of adopting provocative attitudes, eccentric. Addicted to the esoteric, he has been influenced by the poetry of many different countries and ages, for instance Provençal and Chinese. Once leader of the Imagist movement, he has since see-sawed between the scholarly and the sophisticated, the neatly conversational and the mordantly satirical. His most important work so far is his still unfinished *Cantos,* a polyphonic poem constantly shifting from level to level in space and time, sometimes rather laboured and prosaic but with lines of wild and exciting beauty.

Edith Sitwell has experimented along other paths, particularly in the fusion of visual and auditory effects. She transmutes the impressions of a hyperaesthetic sensibility into hard, bright images, organized in a sort of musical masquerade. She has become more and more fascinated by the skeleton beneath the flesh, the worm in the rose, and death now lurks wherever she looks. Her latest poems are more directly emotional, leaping with the fires of the London *blitz.*

About fifteen years ago, Auden, Day Lewis, and Spender launched the new poetry of the thirties. Politically radical and approaching world events analytically, their aim was to create a new vocabulary for a new social consciousness. They drew their material from popular science and the press, from Marx and Freud, from advertisements and jazz. The result was a kind of dynamic reporting in verse form, expressing the troubled awareness of social disintegration and imminent disaster.

W. H. Auden was the boy genius, vital, animated, deeply interested in every human type and every form of life, a mixture of technical virtuoso, mass-observer, magician, psychiatrist, self-centred exhibitionist, and prophet of disaster. Hitherto his flexibility has prevented him from achieving the concentration and perfection of which he gave promise, but he has been a most lively source of stimulus to other poets.

Cecil Day Lewis is a moralist and satirist, a eulogist of rural life and a sharp critic of the stagnant industrial community of the period. His aim is to discover and harness the latent volitional and emotional forces which would make a reconstruction of society possible. Stephen Spender is a pure poet with great organic sensibility, always trying to put himself at the service of society, to reconcile his innate individualism with the necessity for a collective outlook. The difficulty he has felt in harmonizing a sensitive conscience with the will and necessity to act, to intervene effectively in the present state of affairs, has given great dramatic intensity to a poetry rich in clear images and passionate ecstasies.

Louis MacNeice is less closely associated with this group. A liberal of Irish descent he writes in a matter-of-fact, disciplined, conversational tone of the present dilemma of the middle classes, their nostalgic sense of solidarity with what is doomed and disappearing, their fear of upheaval, of the future. Next come two distinctly intellectual poets, William Empson and Ronald Bottrall, both of whom have been influenced by their life abroad and reflect cosmopolitan views. Empson writes a kind of conundrum verse which he has also expounded in theory: he thinks the reading of poetry should be a sort of advanced crossword solving with intricate mental combinations and association patterns. Bottrall is also an enigmatic poet, analytic and very abstract.

Dylan Thomas represents another current in the English poetry of the thirties: the fantastic and myth-making. His Welsh provincialism is fused with a sort of personal surrealism, a fertile imagination mixing biblical allusions and psychoanalytic ideas, folklore and modern neurasthenia, and so charging the blend with sexuality that his whole world becomes a sexual myth. In this particular genre he was a master from the start, an astonishing natural poet, but as yet he has not shown himself capable of any real development.

George Barker has a good deal in common with Thomas. He too cultivates a kind of personal surrealism, producing an abundant flow of verse always focussed on fear and love and coloured by religious mysticism. David Gascoyne, the youngest of these twelve poets, began writing under the influence of French surrealism, but in his first collected volume, *Poems 1937—1942*, he is primarily a follower of the modern French Catholic poets, elegiac and darkly visionary.

In choosing the poems my object has been to give as complete an idea of each poet as possible. Instead of the obvious anthology pieces I have sometimes chosen poems less well known but of equal merit. This applies particularly to Eliot, whose *Prufrock* and *Waste Land* I have excluded. I am sorry that none of the poems in *Four Quartets* could be included: Eliot wishes the work to be treated as a whole and does not permit separate publication of any of its parts.

A. L.

TABLE OF CONTENTS

T. S. ELIOT

PRELUDES

I

The winter evening settles down
With smell of steaks in passageways.
Six o'clock.
The burnt-out ends of smoky days.
And now a gusty shower wraps
The grimy scraps
Of withered leaves about your feet
And newspapers from vacant lots;
The showers beat
On broken blinds and chimney-pots,
And at the corner of the street
A lonely cab-horse steams and stamps.
And then the lighting of the lamps.

II

The morning comes to consciousness
Of faint stale smells of beer
From the sawdust-trampled street
With all its muddy feet that press
To early coffee-stands.

With the other masquerades
That time resumes,
One thinks of all the hands
That are raising dingy shades
In a thousand furnished rooms.

III

You tossed a blanket from the bed,
You lay upon your back, and waited;
You dozed, and watched the night revealing
The thousand sordid images
Of which your soul was constituted
They flickered against the ceiling.
And when all the world came back
And the light crept up between the shutters
And you heard the sparrows in the gutters,
You had such a vision of the street
As the street hardly understands;
Sitting along the bed's edge, where
You curled the papers from your hair,
Or clasped the yellow soles of feet
In the palms of both soiled hands.

IV

His soul stretched tight across the skies
That fade behind a city block,
Or trampled by insistent feet
At four and five and six o'clock;
And short square fingers stuffing pipes,

And evening newspapers, and eyes
Assured of certain certainties,
The conscience of a blackened street
Impatient to assume the world.

I am moved by fancies that are curled
Around these images, and cling:
The notion of some infinitely gentle
Infinitely suffering thing.

Wipe your hand across your mouth, and laugh;
The worlds revolve like ancient women
Gathering fuel in vacant lots.

PORTRAIT OF A LADY

Thou hast committed—
Fornication: but that was in another country,
And besides, the wench is dead.

The Jew of Malta

I

Among the smoke and fog of a December afternoon
You have the scene arrange itself—as it will seem to do—
With 'I have saved this afternoon for you';
And four wax candles in the darkened room,
Four rings of light upon the ceiling overhead,
An atmosphere of Juliet's tomb
Prepared for all the things to be said, or left unsaid.
We have been, let us say, to hear the latest Pole
Transmit the Preludes, through his hair and finger-tips.

'So intimate, this Chopin, that I think his soul
Should be resurrected only among friends
Some two or three, who will not touch the bloom
That is rubbed and questioned in the concert room.'
—And so the conversation slips
Among velleities and carefully caught regrets
Through attenuated tones of violins
Mingled with remote cornets
And begins.
'You do not know how much they mean to me, my friends,
And how, how rare and strange it is, to find
In a life composed so much, so much of odds and ends,
[For indeed I do not love it ... you knew? you are not
　　　　　　　　　　　　　　　　　blind!
How keen you are!]
To find a friend who has these qualities,
Who has, and gives
Those qualities upon which friendship lives.
How much it means that I say this to you—
Without these friendships—life, what *cauchemar!*'

Among the windings of the violins
And the ariettes
Of cracked cornets
Inside my brain a dull tom-tom begins
Absurdly hammering a prelude of its own,
Capricious monotone
That is at least one definite 'false note.'
—Let us take the air, in a tobacco trance,
Admire the monuments,
Discuss the late events,

Correct our watches by the public clocks.
Then sit for half an hour and drink our bocks.

II

Now that lilacs are in bloom
She has a bowl of lilacs in her room
And twists one in her fingers while she talks.
'Ah, my friend, you do not know, you do not know
What life is, you who hold it in your hands';
(Slowly twisting the lilac stalks)
'You let it flow from you, you let it flow,
And youth is cruel, and has no remorse
And smiles at situations which it cannot see.'
I smile, of course,
And go on drinking tea.
'Yet with these April sunsets, that somehow recall
My buried life, and Paris in the Spring.
I feel immeasurably at peace, and find the world
To be wonderful and youthful, after all.'

The voice returns like the insistent out-of-tune
Of a broken violin on an August afternoon:
'I am always sure that you understand
My feelings, always sure that you feel,
Sure that across the gulf you reach your hand.

You are invulnerable, you have no Achilles' heel.
You will go on, and when you have prevailed
You can say: at this point many a one has failed.
But what have I, but what have I, my friend,

To give you, what can you receive from me?
Only the friendship and the sympathy
Of one about to reach her journey's end.

I shall sit here, serving tea to friends . . . .'

I take my hat: how can I make a cowardly amends
For what she has said to me?
You will see me any morning in the park
Reading the comics and the sporting page.
Particularly I remark
An English countess goes upon the stage.
A Greek was murdered at a Polish dance,
Another bank defaulter has confessed.
I keep my countenance,
I remain self-possessed
Except when a street piano, mechanical and tired
Reiterates some worn-out common song
With the smell of hyacinths across the garden
Recalling things that other people have desired.
Are these ideas right or wrong?

III

The October night comes down; returning as before
Except for a slight sensation of being ill at ease
I mount the stairs and turn the handle of the door
And feel as if I had mounted on my hands and knees.
'And so you are going abroad; and when do you return?
But that's a useless question.
You hardly know when you are coming back,

You will find so much to learn.'
My smile falls heavily among the bric-à-brac.

'Perhaps you can write to me.'
My self-possession flares up for a second;
This is as I had reckoned.
'I have been wondering frequently of late
(But our beginnings never know our ends!)
Why we have not developed into friends.'
I feel like one who smiles, and turning shall remark
Suddenly, his expression in a glass.
My self-possession gutters; we are really in the dark.

'For everybody said so, all our friends,
They all were sure our feelings would relate
So closely! I myself can hardly understand.
We must leave it now to fate.
You will write, at any rate.
Perhaps it is not too late.
I shall sit here, serving tea to friends.'
And I must borrow every changing shape
To find expression ... dance, dance
Like a dancing bear,
Cry like a parrot, chatter like an ape.
Let us take the air, in a tobacco trance—

Well! and what if she should die some afternoon,
Afternoon grey and smoky, evening yellow and rose;
Should die and leave me sitting pen in hand
With the smoke coming down above the housetops;
Doubtful, for a while

Not knowing what to feel or if I understand
Or whether wise or foolish, tardy or too soon ...
Would she not have the advantage, after all?
This music is successful with a 'dying fall'
Now that we talk of dying—
And should I have the right to smile?

GERONTION

> *Thou hast nor youth nor age*
> *But as it were an after dinner sleep*
> *Dreaming of both.*

Here I am, an old man in a dry month,
Being read to by a boy, waiting for rain.
I was neither at the hot gates
Nor fought in the warm rain
Nor knee deep in the salt marsh, heaving a cutlass,
Bitten by flies, fought.
My house is a decayed house,
And the jew squats on the window sill, the owner,
Spawned in some estaminet of Antwerp,
Blistered in Brussels, patched and peeled in London.
The goat coughs at night in the field overhead;
Rocks, moss, stonecrop, iron, merds.
The woman keeps the kitchen, makes tea,
Sneezes at evening, poking the peevish gutter.
                                        I an old man,
A dull head among windy spaces

Signs are taken for wonders. 'We would see a sign!'
The word within a word, unable to speak a word,

Swaddled with darkness. In the juvescence of the year
Came Christ the tiger

In depraved May, dogwood and chestnut, flowering judas,
To be eaten, to be divided, to be drunk
Among whispers; by Mr. Silvero
With caressing hands, at Limoges
Who walked all night in the next room;
By Hakagawa, bowing among the Titians;
By Madame de Tornquist, in the dark room
Shifting the candles; Fräulein von Kulp
Who turned in the hall, one hand on the door. Vacant
                                        shuttles
Weave the wind. I have no ghosts,
An old man in a draughty house
Under a windy knob.

After such knowledge, what forgiveness? Think now
History has many cunning passages, contrived corridors
And issues, deceives with whispering ambitions,
Guides us by vanities. Think now
She gives when our attention is distracted
And what she gives, gives with such supple confusions
That the giving famishes the craving. Gives too late
What's not believed in, or if still believed,
In memory only, reconsidered passion. Gives too soon
Into weak hands, what's thought can be dispensed with
Till the refusal propagates a fear. Think
Neither fear nor courage saves us. Unnatural vices
Are fathered by our heroism. Virtues

Are forced upon us by our impudent crimes.
These tears are shaken from the wrath-bearing tree.

The tiger springs in the new year. Us he devours. Think
                               at last
We have not reached conclusion, when I
Stiffen in a rented house. Think at last
I have not made this show purposelessly
And it is not by any concitation
Of the backward devils.
I would meet you upon this honestly.
I that was near your heart was removed therefrom
To lose beauty in terror, terror in inquisition.
I have lost my passion: why should I need to keep it
Since what is kept must be adulterated?
I have lost my sight, smell, hearing, taste and touch:
How should I use them for your closer contact?

These with a thousand small deliberations
Protract the profit of their chilled delirium,
Excite the membrane, when the sense has cooled,
With pungent sauces, multiply variety
In a wilderness of mirrors. What will the spider do,
Suspend its operations, will the weevil
Delay? De Bailhache, Fresca, Mrs. Cammel, whirled
Beyond the circuit of the shuddering Bear
In fractured atoms. Gull against the wind, in the windy
                               straits
Of Belle Isle, or running on the Horn,
White feathers in the snow, the Gulf claims,

And an old man driven by the Trades
To a sleepy corner.

                              Tenants of the house,
Thoughts of a dry brain in a dry season.

BURBANK WITH A BAEDEKER: BLEISTEIN WITH A CIGAR

> *Tra-la-la-la-la-la-laire—nil nisi divinum stabile
> est; caetera fumus—the gondola stopped, the old
> palace was there, how charming its grey and pink—
> goats and monkeys, with such hair too!—so the
> countess passed on until she came through the little
> park, where Niobe presented her with a cabinet,
> and so departed.*

Burbank crossed a little bridge
    Descending at a small hotel;
Princess Volupine arrived,
    They were together, and he fell.

Defunctive music under sea
    Passed seaward with the passing bell
Slowly: the God Hercules
    Had left him, that had loved him well.

The horses, under the axletree
    Beat up the dawn from Istria
With even feet. Her shuttered barge
    Burned on the water all the day.

But this or such was Bleistein's way:
  A saggy bending of the knees
And elbows, with the palms turned out,
  Chicago Semite Viennese.

A lustreless protrusive eye
  Stares from the protozoic slime
At a perspective of Canaletto.
  The smoky candle end of time

Declines. On the Rialto once.
  The rats are underneath the piles.
The jew is underneath the lot.
  Money in furs. The boatman smiles,

Princess Volupine extends
  A meagre, blue-nailed, phthisic hand
To climb the waterstair. Lights, lights,
  She entertains Sir Ferdinand

Klein. Who clipped the lion's wings
  And flea'd his rump and pared his claws?
Thought Burbank, meditating on
  Time's ruins, and the seven laws.

THE HIPPOPOTAMUS

*And when this epistle is read among you, cause that
it be read also in the church of the Laodiceans.*

The broad-backed hippopotamus
Rests on his belly in the mud;

Although he seems so firm to us
He is merely flesh and blood.

Flesh and blood is weak and frail,
Susceptible to nervous shock;
While the True Church can never fail
For it is based upon a rock.

The hippo's feeble steps may err
In compassing material ends,
While the True Church need never stir
To gather in its dividends.

The 'potamus can never reach
The mango on the mango-tree;
But fruits of pomegranate and peach
Refresh the Church from over sea.

At mating time the hippo's voice
Betrays inflexions hoarse and odd,
But every week we hear rejoice
The Church, at being one with God.

The hippopotamus's day
Is passed in sleep; at night he hunts;
God works in a mysterious way—
The Church can sleep and feed at once.

I saw the 'potamus take wing
Ascending from the damp savannas,

And quiring angels round him sing
The praise of God, in loud hosannas.

Blood of the Lamb shall wash him clean
And him shall heavenly arms enfold,
Among the saints he shall be seen
Performing on a harp of gold.

He shall be washed as white as snow,
By all the martyr'd virgins kist,
While the True Church remains below
Wrapt in the old miasmal mist.

ASH-WEDNESDAY

I

Because I do not hope to turn again
Because I do not hope
Because I do not hope to turn
Desiring this man's gift and that man's scope
I no longer strive to strive towards such things
(Why should the agèd eagle stretch its wings?)
Why should I mourn
The vanished power of the usual reign?

Because I do not hope to know again
The infirm glory of the positive hour
Because I do not think
Because I know I shall not know

The one veritable transitory power
Because I cannot drink
There, where trees flower, and springs flow, for there is
                                        nothing again

Because I know that time is always time
And place is always and only place
And what is actual is actual only for one time
And only for one place
I rejoice that things are as they are and
I renounce the blessèd face
And renounce the voice
Because I cannot hope to turn again
Consequently I rejoice, having to construct something
Upon which to rejoice

And pray to God to have mercy upon us
And I pray that I may forget
These matters that with myself I too much discuss
Too much explain
Because I do not hope to turn again
Let these words answer
For what is done, not to be done again
May the judgement not be too heavy upon us

Because these wings are no longer wings to fly
But merely vans to beat the air
The air which is now thoroughly small and dry
Smaller and dryer than the will
Teach us to care and not to care
Teach us to sit still.

Pray for us sinners now and at the hour of our death
Pray for us now and at the hour of our death.

II

Lady, three white leopards sat under a juniper-tree
In the cool of the day, having fed to satiety
On my legs my heart my liver and that which had been
                               contained
In the hollow round of my skull. And God said
Shall these bones live? shall these
Bones live? And that which had been contained
In the bones (which were already dry) said chirping:
Because of the goodness of this Lady
And because of her loveliness, and because
She honours the Virgin in meditation,
We shine with brightness. And I who am here dissembled
Proffer my deeds to oblivion, and my love
To the posterity of the desert and the fruit of the gourd.
It is this which recovers
My guts the strings of my eyes and the indigestible
                               portions
Which the leopards reject. The Lady is withdrawn
In a white gown, to contemplation, in a white gown.
Let the whiteness of bones atone to forgetfulness.
There is no life in them. As I am forgotten
And would be forgotten, so I would forget
Thus devoted, concentrated in purpose. And God said
Prophesy to the wind, to the wind only for only
The wind will listen. And the bones sang chirping
With the burden of the grasshopper, saying

Lady of silences
Calm and distressed
Torn and most whole
Rose of memory
Rose of forgetfulness
Exhausted and life-giving
Worried reposeful
The single Rose
Is now the Garden
Where all loves end
Terminate torment
Of love unsatisfied
The greater torment
Of love satisfied
End of the endless
Journey to no end
Conclusion of all that
Is inconclusible
Speech without word and
Word of no speech
Grace to the Mother
For the Garden
Where all love ends.

Under a juniper-tree the bones sang, scattered and shining
We are glad to be scattered, we did little good to each
                                        other,
Under a tree in the cool of the day, with the blessing of
                                        sand,
Forgetting themselves and each other, united
In the quiet of the desert. This is the land which ye

Shall divide by lot. And neither division nor unity
Matters. This is the land. We have our inheritance.

III

At the first turning of the second stair
I turned and saw below
The same shape twisted on the banister
Under the vapour in the fetid air
Struggling with the devil of the stairs who wears
The deceitful face of hope and of despair.

At the second turning of the second stair
I left them twisting, turning below;
There were no more faces and the stair was dark,
Damp, jaggèd, like an old man's mouth drivelling,
                           beyond repair,
Or the toothed gullet of an agèd shark.

At the first turning of the third stair
Was a slotted window bellied like the fig's fruit
And beyond the hawthorn blossom and a pasture scene
The broadbacked figure drest in blue and green
Enchanted the maytime with an antique flute.
Blown hair is sweet, brown hair over the mouth blown,
Lilac and brown hair;
Distraction, music of the flute, stops and steps of the mind
                          over the third stair,
Fading, fading; strength beyond hope and despair
Climbing the third stair.

Lord, I am not worthy
Lord, I am not worthy

     but speak the word only.

IV

Who walked between the violet and the violet
Who walked between
The various ranks of varied green
Going in white and blue, in Mary's colour,
Talking of trivial things
In ignorance and in knowledge of eternal dolour
Who moved among the others as they walked,
Who then made strong the fountains and made fresh the
                     springs

Made cool the dry rock and made firm the sand
In blue of larkspur, blue of Mary's colour,
Sovegna vos

Here are the years that walk between, bearing
Away the fiddles and the flutes, restoring
One who moves in the time between sleep and waking,
                   wearing

White light folded, sheathed about her, folded.
The new years walk, restoring
Through a bright cloud of tears, the years, restoring
With a new verse the ancient rhyme. Redeem
The time. Redeem

The unread vision in the higher dream
While jewelled unicorns draw by the gilded hearse.

The silent sister veiled in white and blue
Between the yews, behind the garden god,
Whose flute is breathless, bent her head and signed but
                                          spoke no word

But the fountain sprang up and the bird sang down
Redeem the time, redeem the dream
The token of the word unheard, unspoken

Till the wind shake a thousand whispers from the yew

And after this our exile

V

If the lost word is lost, if the spent word is spent
If the unheard, unspoken
Word is unspoken, unheard;
Still is the unspoken word, the Word unheard,
The Word without a word, the Word within
The world and for the world;
And the light shone in darkness and
Against the World the unstilled world still whirled
About the centre of the silent Word.

O my people, what have I done unto thee.

Where shall the word be found, where will the word
Resound? Not here, there is not enough silence

Not on the sea or on the islands, not
On the mainland, in the desert or the rain land,
For those who walk in darkness
Both in the day time and in the night time
The right time and the right place are not here
No place of grace for those who avoid the face
No time to rejoice for those who walk among noise and
                              deny the voice

Will the veiled sister pray for
Those who walk in darkness, who chose thee and oppose
                              thee,
Those who are torn on the horn between season and
                              season, time and time, between
Hour and hour, word and word, power and power, those
                              who wait
In darkness? Will the veiled sister pray
For children at the gate
Who will not go away and cannot pray:
Pray for those who chose and oppose

        O my people, what have I done unto thee.

Will the veiled sister between the slender
Yew trees pray for those who offend her
And are terrified and cannot surrender
And affirm before the world and deny between the rocks
In the last desert between the last blue rocks
The desert in the garden the garden in the desert
Of drouth, spitting from the mouth the withered apple-
                              seed.

        O my people.

VI

Although I do not hope to turn again
Although I do not hope
Although I do not hope to turn

Wavering between the profit and the loss
In this brief transit where the dreams cross
The dreamcrossed twilight between birth and dying
(Bless me father) though I do not wish to wish these things
From the wide window towards the granite shore
The white sails still fly seaward, seaward flying
Unbroken wings

And the lost heart stiffens and rejoices
In the lost lilac and the lost sea voices
And the weak spirit quickens to rebel
For the bent golden-rod and the lost sea smell
Quickens to recover
The cry of quail and the whirling plover
And the blind eye creates
The empty forms between the ivory gates
And smell renews the salt savour of the sandy earth

This is the time of tension between dying and birth
The place of solitude where three dreams cross
Between blue rocks
But when the voices shaken from the yew-tree drift away
Let the other yew be shaken and reply.
Blessèd sister, holy mother, spirit of the fountain, spirit
                                        of the garden,

Suffer us not to mock ourselves with falsehood
Teach us to care and not to care
Teach us to sit still
Even among these rocks,
Our peace in His will
And even among these rocks
Sister, mother
And spirit of the river, spirit of the sea,
Suffer me not to be separated

And let my cry come unto Thee.

MARINA

*Quis hic locus, quae
regio, quae mundi plaga.*

What seas what shores what grey rocks and what islands
What water lapping the bow
And scent of pine and the woodthrush singing through the
fog
What images return
O my daughter.

Those who sharpen the tooth of the dog, meaning
Death
Those who glitter with the glory of the hummingbird,
meaning
Death
Those who sit in the stye of contentment, meaning
Death
Those who suffer the ecstasy of the animals, meaning
Death

Are become unsubstantial, reduced by a wind,
A breath of pine, and the woodsong fog
By this grace dissolved in place

What is this face, less clear and clearer
The pulse in the arm, less strong and stronger—
Given or lent? more distant than stars and nearer than
                           the eye

Whispers and small laughter between leaves and hurrying
                         feet
Under sleep, where all the waters meet.

Bowsprit cracked with ice and paint cracked with heat.
I made this, I have forgotten
And remember.
The rigging weak and the canvas rotten
Between one June and another September.
Made this unknowing, half conscious, unknown, my own.
The garboard strake leaks, the seams need caulking.
This form, this face, this life
Living to live in a world of time beyond me; let me
Resign my life for this life, my speech for that unspoken,
The awakened, lips parted, the hope, the new ships.

What seas what shores what granite islands towards my
                         timbers
And woodthrush calling through the fog
My daughter.

LANDSCAPES

USK

Do not suddenly break the branch, or
Hope to find
The white hart behind the white well.
Glance aside, not for lance, do not spell
Old enchantments. Let them sleep.
'Gently dip, but not too deep',
Lift your eyes
Where the roads dip and where the roads rise
Seek only there
Where the grey light meets the green air
The hermit's chapel, the pilgrim's prayer.

RANNOCH, BY GLENCOE

Here the crow starves, here patient stag
Breeds for the rifle. Between the soft moor
And the soft sky, scarcely room
To leap or soar. Substance crumbles, in the thin air
Moon cold or moon hot. The road winds in
Listlessness of ancient war,
Languor of broken steel,
Clamour of confused wrong, apt
In silence. Memory is strong
Beyond the bone. Pride snapped,
Shadow of pride is long, in the long pass
No concurrence of bone.

LITTLE GIDDING

I

Midwinter spring is its own season
Sempiternal though sodden towards sundown,
Suspended in time, between pole and tropic.
When the short day is brightest, with frost and fire,
The brief sun flames the ice, on pond and ditches,
In windless cold that is the heart's heat,
Reflecting in a watery mirror
A glare that is blindness in the early afternoon.
And glow more intense than blaze of branch, or brazier,
Stirs the dumb spirit: no wind, but pentecostal fire
In the dark time of the year. Between melting and
                                        freezing
The soul's sap quivers. There is no earth smell
Or smell of living thing. This is the spring time
But not in time's covenant. Now the hedgerow
Is blanched for an hour with transitory blossom
Of snow, a bloom more sudden
Than that of summer, neither budding nor fading,
Not in the scheme of generation.
Where is the summer, the unimaginable
Zero summer?

If you came this way,
Taking the route you would be likely to take
From the place you would be likely to come from,
If you came this way in may time, you would find the
                                        hedges

White again, in May, with voluptuary sweetness.
It would be the same at the end of the journey,
If you came at night like a broken king,
If you came by day not knowing what you came for,
It would be the same, when you leave the rough road
And turn behind the pig-sty to the dull façade
And the tombstone. And what you thought you came for
Is only a shell, a husk of meaning
From which the purpose breaks only when it is fulfilled
If at all. Either you had no purpose
Or the purpose is beyond the end you figured
And is altered in fulfilment. There are other places
Which also are the world's end, some at the sea jaws,
Or over a dark lake, in a desert or a city—
But this is the nearest, in place and time,
Now and in England.

        If you came this way,
Taking any route, starting from anywhere,
At any time or at any season,
It would always be the same: you would have to put off
Sense and notion. You are not here to verify,
Instruct yourself, or inform curiosity
Or carry report. You are here to kneel
Where prayer has been valid. And prayer is more
Than an order of words, the conscious occupation
Of the praying mind, or the sound of the voice praying.
And what the dead had no speech for, when living,
They can tell you, being dead: the communication
Of the dead is tongued with fire beyond the language
                        of the living.

Here, the intersection of the timeless moment
Is England and nowhere. Never and always.

II

Ash on an old man's sleeve
Is all the ash the burnt roses leave.
Dust in the air suspended
Marks the place where a story ended.
Dust inbreathed was a house—
The wall, the wainscot and the mouse.
The death of hope and despair,
        This is the death of air.

There are flood and drouth
Over the eyes and in the mouth,
Dead water and dead sand
Contending for the upper hand.
The parched eviscerate soil
Gapes at the vanity of toil,
Laughs without mirth.
        This is the death of earth.

Water and fire succeed
The town, the pasture and the weed.
Water and fire deride
The sacrifice that we denied.
Water and fire shall rot
The marred foundations we forgot,
Of sanctuary and choir.
        This is the death of water and fire.

In the uncertain hour before the morning
  Near the ending of interminable night
  At the recurrent end of the unending
After the dark dove with the flickering tongue
  Had passed below the horizon of his homing
  While the dead leaves still rattled on like tin
Over the asphalt where no other sound was
  Between three districts whence the smoke arose
  I met one walking, loitering and hurried
As if blown towards me like the metal leaves
  Before the urban dawn wind unresisting.
  And as I fixed upon the down-turned face
That pointed scrutiny with which we challenge
  The first-met stranger in the waning dusk
  I caught the sudden look of some dead master
Whom I had known, forgotten, half recalled
  Both one and many; in the brown baked features
  They eyes of a familiar compound ghost
Both intimate and unidentifiable.
  So I assumed a double part, and cried
  And heard another's voice cry: 'What! are *you* here?'
Although we were not. I was still the same,
  Knowing myself yet being someone other—
  And he a face still forming; yet the words sufficed
To compel the recognition they preceded.
  And so, compliant to the common wind,
  Too strange to each other for misunderstanding,
In concord at this intersection time
  Of meeting nowhere, no before and after,
  We trod the pavement in a dead patrol.
I said: 'The wonder that I feel is easy,

Yet ease is cause of wonder. Therefore speak:
I may not comprehend, may not remember.'
And he: 'I am not eager to rehearse
My thought and theory which you have forgotten.
These things have served their purpose: let them be.
So with your own, and pray they be forgiven
By others, as I pray you to forgive
Both bad and good. Last season's fruit is eaten
And the fullfed beast shall kick the empty pail.
For last year's words belong to last year's language
And next year's words await another voice.
But, as the passage now presents no hindrance
To the spirit unappeased and peregrine
Between two worlds become much like each other,
So I find words I never thought to speak
In streets I never thought I should revisit
When I left my body on a distant shore.
Since our concern was speech, and speech impelled us
To purify the dialect of the tribe
And urge the mind to aftersight and foresight,
Let me disclose the gifts reserved for age
To set a crown upon your lifetime's effort.
First, the cold friction of expiring sense
Without enchantment, offering no promise
But bitter tastelessness of shadow fruit
As body and soul begin to fall asunder.
Second, the conscious impotence of rage
At human folly, and the laceration
Of laughter at what ceases to amuse.
And last, the rending pain of re-enactment
Of all that you have done, and been; the shame

Of motives late revealed, and the awareness
Of things ill done and done to others' harm
  Which once you took for exercise of virtue.
  Then fools' approval stings, and honour stain..
From wrong to wrong the exasperated spirit
  Proceeds, unless restored by that refining fire
  Where you must move in measure, like a dancer.'
The day was breaking. In the disfigured street
  He left me, with a kind of valediction,
  And faded on the blowing of the horn.

III

There are three conditions which often look alike
Yet differ completely, flourish in the same hedgerow:
Attachment to self and to things and to persons,
                    detachment
From self and from things and from persons; and,
                    growing between them, indifference
Which resembles the others as death resembles life,
Being between two lives—unflowering, between
The live and the dead nettle. This is the use of memory:
For liberation—not less of love but expanding
Of love beyond desire, and so liberation
From the future as well as the past. Thus, love of a
                    country
Begins as attachment to our own field of action
And comes to find that action of little importance
Though never indifferent. History may be servitude,
History may be freedom. See, now they vanish,

The faces and places, with the self which, as it could,
               loved them,
To become renewed, transfigured, in another pattern.
Sin is Behovely, but
All shall be well, and
All manner of thing shall be well.
If I think, again, of this place,
And of people, not wholly commendable,
Of no immediate kin or kindness,
But some of peculiar genius,
All touched by a common genius,
United in the strife which divided them;
If I think of a king at nightfall,
Of three men, and more, on the scaffold
And a few who died forgotten
In other places, here and abroad,
And of one who died blind and quiet,
Why should we celebrate
These dead men more than the dying?
It is not to ring the bell backward
Nor is it an incantation
To summon the spectre of a Rose.
We cannot revive old factions
We cannot restore old policies
Or follow an antique drum.
These men, and those who opposed them
And those whom they opposed
Accept the constitution of silence
And are folded in a single party.
Whatever we inherit from the fortunate
We have taken from the defeated

What they had to leave us—a symbol:
A symbol perfected in death.
And all shall be well and
All manner of thing shall be well
By the purification of the motive
In the ground of our beseeching.

IV

The dove descending breaks the air
With flame of incandescent terror
Of which the tongues declare
The one discharge from sin and error.
The only hope, or else despair
   Lies in the choice of pyre or pyre—
   To be redeemed from fire by fire.

Who then devised the torment? Love.
Love is the unfamiliar Name
Behind the hands that wove
The intolerable shirt of flame
Which human power cannot remove.
   We only live, only suspire
   Consumed by either fire or fire.

V

What we call the beginning is often the end
And to make an end is to make a beginning.
The end is where we start from. And every phrase
And sentence that is right (where every word is at home,

Taking its place to support the others,
The word neither diffident nor ostentatious,
An easy commerce of the old and the new,
The common word exact without vulgarity,
The formal word precise but not pedantic,
The complete consort dancing together)
Every phrase and every sentence is an end and a
                                 beginning,
Every poem an epitaph. And any action
Is a step to the block, to the fire, down the sea's throat
Or to an illegible stone: and that is where we start.
We die with the dying:
See, they depart, and we go with them.
We are born with the dead:
See, they return, and bring us with them.
The moment of the rose and the moment of the yew-tree
Are of equal duration. A people without history
Is not redeemed from time, for history is a pattern
Of timeless moments. So, while the light fails
On a winter's afternoon, in a secluded chapel
History is now and England.

With the drawing of this Love and the voice of this
                                 Calling

We shall not cease from exploration
And the end of all our exploring
Will be to arrive where we started
And know the place for the first time.
Through the unknown, remembered gate

When the last of earth left to discover
Is that which was the beginning;
At the source of the longest river
The voice of the hidden waterfall
And the children in the apple-tree
Not known, because not looked for
But heard, half-heard, in the stillness
Between two waves of the sea.
Quick now, here, now, always—
A condition of complete simplicity
(Costing not less than everything)
And all shall be well and
All manner of thing shall be well
When the tongues of flame are in-folded
Into the crowned knot of fire
And the fire and the rose are one.

EZRA POUND

PARACELSUS IN EXCELSIS

"Being no longer human, why should I
Pretend humanity or don the frail attire?
Men have I known and men, but never one
Was grown so free an essence, or become
So simply element as what I am.
The mist goes from the mirror and I see.
Behold! the world of forms is swept beneath—
Turmoil grown visible beneath our peace,
And we that are grown formless, rise above—
Fluids intangible that have been men,
We seem as statues round whose high-risen base
Some overflowing river is run mad,
In us alone the element of calm."

FRANCESCA

You came in out of the night
And there were flowers in your hands,
Now you will come out of a confusion of people,
Out of a turmoil of speech about you.

I who have seen you amid the primal things
Was angry when they spoke your name
In ordinary places.
I would that the cool waves might flow over my mind,
And that the world should dry as a dead leaf,
Or as a dandelion seed-pod and be swept away,
So that I might find you again,
Alone.

THE NEEDLE

Come, or the stellar tide will slip away.
Eastward avoid the hour of its decline,
Now! for the needle trembles in my soul!

Here have we had our vantage, the good hour.
Here we have had our day, your day and mine.
Come now, before this power
That bears us up, shall turn against the pole.

Mock not the flood of stars, the thing's to be.
O Love, come now, this land turns evil slowly.
The waves bore in, soon will they bear away.

The treasure is ours, make we fast land with it.
Move we and take the tide, with its next favour,
Abide
Under some neutral force
Until this course turneth aside.

THE PLUNGE

I would bathe myself in strangeness:
These comforts heaped upon me, smother me!
I burn, I scald so for the new,
New friends, new faces,
Places!
Oh to be out of this,
This that is all I wanted
        —save the new.

And you,
Love, you the much, the more desired!
Do I not loathe all walls, streets, stones,
All mire, mist, all fog,
All ways of traffic?
You, I would have flow over me like water,
Oh, but far out of this!
Grass, and low fields, and hills,
And sun,
Oh, sun enough!
Out, and alone, among some
Alien people!

ORTUS

How have I laboured?
How have I not laboured
To bring her soul to birth,
To give these elements a name and a centre!
She is beautiful as the sunlight, and as fluid.

She has no name, and no place.
How have I laboured to bring her soul into separation;
To give her a name and her being!

Surely you are bound and entwined,
You are mingled with the elements unborn;
I have loved a stream and a shadow.

I beseech you enter your life.
I beseech you learn to say "I,"
When I question you;
For you are no part, but a whole,
No portion, but a being.

SALUTATION

O generation of the thoroughly smug
        and thoroughly uncomfortable,
I have seen fishermen picnicking in the sun,
I have seen them with untidy families,
I have seen their smiles full of teeth
        and heard ungainly laughter.
And I am happier than you are,
And they were happier than I am;
And the fish swim in the lake
        and do not even own clothing.

COMMISSION

Go, my songs, to the lonely and the unsatisfied,
Go also to the nerve-wracked, go to the enslaved-by-
                                    convention,

Bear to them my contempt for their oppressors.
Go as a great wave of cool water,
Bear my contempt of oppressors.

Speak against unconscious oppression,
Speak against the tyranny of the unimaginative,
Speak against bonds.
Go to the bourgeoise who is dying of her ennuis,
Go to the women in suburbs.
Go to the hideously wedded,
Go to them whose failure is concealed,
Go to the unluckily mated,
Go to the bought wife,
Go to the woman entailed.

Go to those who have delicate lust,
Go to those whose delicate desires are thwarted,
Go like a blight upon the dulness of the world;
Go with your edge against this,
Strengthen the subtle cords,
Bring confidence upon the algæ and the tentacles of the
                                         soul.

Go in a friendly manner,
Go with an open speech.
Be eager to find new evils and new good,
Be against all forms of oppression.
Go to those who are thickened with middle age,
To those who have lost their interest.

Go to the adolescent who are smothered in family—
Oh how hideous it is

To see three generations of one house gathered together!
It is like an old tree with shoots,
And with some branches rotted and falling.

Go out and defy opinion,
Go against this vegetable bondage of the blood.
Be against all sorts of mortmain.

DANCE FIGURE

For the Marriage in Cana of Galilee

Dark eyed,
O woman of my dreams,
Ivory sandaled,
There is none like thee among the dancers,
None with swift feet.

I have not found thee in the tents,
In the broken darkness.
I have not found thee at the well-head
Among the women with pitchers.

Thine arms are as a young sapling under the bark;
Thy face as a river with lights.

White as an almond are thy shoulders;
As new almonds stripped from the husk.
They guard thee not with eunuchs;
Not with bars of copper.

Gilt turquoise and silver are in the place of thy rest.
A brown robe, with threads of gold woven in patterns,
                hast thou gathered about thee,
O Nathat-Ikanaie, "Tree-at-the-river."

As a rillet among the sedge are thy hands upon me;
Thy fingers a frosted stream.

Thy maidens are white like pebbles;
Their music about thee!

There is none like thee among the dancers;
None with swift feet.

NEAR PERIGORD

III

Ed eran due in uno, ed uno in due;
Inferno, XXVIII, 125

Bewildering spring, and by the Auvezere
       Poppies and day's eyes in the green émail
      Rose over us; and we knew all that stream,
And our two horses had traced out the valleys;
Knew the low flooded lands squared out with poplars,
In the young days when the deep sky befriended.
      And great wings beat above us in the twilight,
And the great wheels in heaven
Bore us together ... surging ... and apart ...
Believing we should meet with lips and hands,

High, high and sure ... and then the counterthrust:
'Why do you love me? Will you always love me?
But I am like the grass, I can not love you.'
Or, 'Love, and I love and love you,
And hate your mind, not *you*, your soul, your hands.'

.   So to this last estrangement, Tairiran!

There shut up in his castle, Tairiran's,
She who had nor ears nor tongue save in her hands,
Gone—ah, gone—untouched, unreachable!
She who could never live save through one person,
She who could never speak save to one person,
And all the rest of her a shifting change,
A broken bundle of mirrors ... !

MAUBERLEY

IV

Scattered Moluccas
Not knowing, day to day,
The first day's end, in the next noon;
The placid water
Unbroken by the Simoon;

Thick foliage
Placid beneath warm suns,
Tawn fore-shores
Washed in the cobalt of oblivions;

Or through dawn-mist
The grey and rose
Of the juridical
Flamingoes;

A consciousness disjunct,
Being but this overblotted
Series
Of intermittences;

Coracle of Pacific voyages,
The unforecasted beach;
Then on an oar
Read this:

"I was
And I no more exist;
Here drifted
An hedonist."

CANTOS

II

Hang it all, Robert Browning,
          there can be but the one 'Sordello'.
But Sordello, and my Sordello?
Lo Sordels si fo di Mantovana.
So-shu churned in the sea.
Seal sports in the spray-whited circles of cliff-wash,
Sleek head, daughter of Lir,
          eyes of Picasso

Under black fur-hood, lithe daughter of Ocean;
And the wave runs in the beach-groove:
'Eleanor, ἑλέναυς and ἑλέπτολις!'
                    And poor old Homer blind, blind, as a bat,
Ear, ear for the sea-surge, murmur of old men's voices:
'Let her go back the ships,
Back among Grecian faces, lest evil come on our own,
Evil and further evil, and a curse cursed on our children,
Moves, yes she moves like a goddess
And has the face of a god
                    and the voice of Schoeney's daughters,
And doom goes with her in walking,
Let her go back to the ships,
                    back among Grecian voices.'
And by the beach-run, Tyro,
                    Twisted arms of the sea-god,
Lithe sinews of water, gripping her, cross-hold,
And the blue-gray glass of the wave tents them,
Glare azure of water, cold-welter, close cover.
Quiet sun-tawny sand-stretch,
The gulls broad out their wings,
                    nipping between the splay feathers;
Snipe come for their bath,
                    bend out their wing-joints,
Spread wet wings to the sun-film,
And by Scios,
                    to left of the Naxos passage,
Naviform rock overgrown,
                    algæ cling to its edge,
There is a wine-red glow in the shallows,
                    a tin flash in the sun-dazzle.

The ship landed in Scios,
   men wanting spring-water,
And by the rock-pool a young boy loggy with vine-must,
   'To Naxos? Yes, we'll take you to Naxos,
Cum' along lad.' 'Not that way!'
'Aye, that way is Naxos.'
     And I said: 'It's a straight ship.'
And an ex-convict out of Italy
   knocked me into the fore-stays,
(He was wanted for manslaughter in Tuscany)
   And the whole twenty against me,
Mad for a little slave money.
   And they took her out of Scios
And off her course . . .
   And the boy came to, again, with the racket,
And looked out over the bows,
   and to eastward, and to the Naxos passage.
God-sleight then, god-sleight:
   Ship stock fast in sea-swirl,
Ivy upon the oars, King Pentheus,
   grapes with no seed but sea-foam,
Ivy in scupper-hole.
Aye, I, Accœtes, stood there,
   and the god stood by me,
Water cutting under the keel,
Sea-break from stern forrards,
   wake running off from the bow,
And where was gunwale, there now was vine-trunk,
And tenthril where cordage had been,
   grape-leaves on the rowlocks,
Heavy vine on the oarshafts,

And, out of nothing, a breathing,
        hot breath on my ankles,
Beasts like shadows in glass,
        a furred tail upon nothingness.
Lynx-purr, and heathery smell of beasts,
        where tar smell had been,
Sniff and pad-foot of beasts,
        eye-glitter out of black air.
The sky overshot, dry, with no tempest,
Sniff and pad-foot of beasts,
        fur brushing my knee-skin,
Rustle of airy sheaths,
        dry forms in the *æther*.
And the ship like a keel in ship-yard,
        slung like an ox in smith's sling,
Ribs stuck fast in the ways,
        grape-cluster over pin-rack,
        void air taking pelt.
Lifeless air become sinewed,
        feline leisure of panthers,
Leopards sniffing the grape shoots by scupper-hole,
Crouched panthers by fore-hatch,
And the sea blue-deep about us,
        green-ruddy in shadows,
And Lyæus: 'From now, Acœtes, my altars,
Fearing no bondage,
        Fearing no cat of the wood,
Safe with my lynxes,
        feeding grapes to my leopards,
Olibanum is my incense,
        the vines grow in my homage.'

The back-swell now smooth in the rudder-chains,
Black snout of a porpoise
       where Lycabs had been,
Fish-scales on the oarsmen.
       And I worship.
I have seen what I have seen.
       When they brought the boy I said:
'He has a god in him,
       though I do not know which god.'
And they kicked me into the fore-stays.
I have seen what I have seen:
       Medon's face like the face of a dory,
Arms shrunk into fins. And you, Pentheus,
Had as well listen to Tiresias, and to Cadmus,
       or your luck will go out of you.
Fish-scales over groin muscles,
       lynx-purr amid sea...
And of a later year,
       pale in the wine-red algæ,
If you will lean over the rock,
       the coral face under wave-tinge,
Rose-paleness under water-shift,
       Ileuthyeria, fair Dafne of sea-bords,
The swimmer's arms turned to branches,
Who will say in what year,
       fleeing what band of tritons,
The smooth brows, seen, and half seen,
       now ivory stillness.
And So-shu churned in the sea, So-shu also,
       using the long moon for a churn-stick...

Lithe turning of water,
            sinews of Poseidon,
Black azure and hyaline,
            glass wave over Tyro,
Close cover, unstillness,
            bright welter of wave-cords,
Then quiet water,
            quiet in the buff sands,
Sea-fowl stretching wing-joints,
            splashing in rock-hollows and sand-hollows
In the wave-runs by the half-dune;
Glass-glint of wave in the tide-rips against sunlight,
            pallor of Hesperus,
Grey peak of the wave,
            wave, colour of grape's pulp,

Olive grey in the near,
            far, smoke grey of the rock-slide,
Salmon-pink wings of the fish-hawk
            cast grey shadows in water,
The tower like a one-eyed great goose
            cranes up out of the olive-grove,

And we have heard the fauns chiding Proteus
            in the smell of hay under the olive-trees,
And the frogs singing against the fauns
            in the half-light.
And . . .

XLVII

Who even dead, yet hath his mind entire!
This sound came in the dark
First must thou go the road
                              to hell
And to the bower of Ceres' daughter Proserpine,
Through overhanging dark, to see Tiresias,
Eyeless that was, a shade, that is in hell
So full of knowing that the beefy men know less than he,
Ere thou come to thy road's end.
                    Knowledge the shade of a shade,
Yet must thou sail after knowledge
Knowing less than drugged beasts. *phtheggometha
thasson*
φθεγγώμεθα θᾶσσον
            The small lamps drift in the bay
And the sea's claw gathers them.
Neptunus drinks after neap-tide.
Tamuz! Tamuz!!
The red flame going seaward.
            By this gate art thou measured.
From the long boats they have set lights in the water,
The sea's claw gathers them outward.
Scilla's dogs snarl at the cliff's base,
The white teeth gnaw in under the crag,
But in the pale night the small lamps float seaward
                                        τυ Διώνα
                                        TU DIONA

και Μοῖρα τ᾽ Ἄδονιν
KAI MOIRA T' ADONIN

The sea is streaked red with Adonis,
The lights flicker red in small jars.
Wheat shoots rise new by the altar,
    flower from the swift seed.
Two span, two span to a woman,
Beyond that she believes not. Nothing is of any impor-
                          tance.
To that is she bent, her intention,
To that art thou called ever turning intention,
Whether by night the owl-call, whether by sap in shoot,
Never idle, by no means by no wiles intermittent
Moth is called over mountain
The bull runs blind on the sword, *naturans*
To the cave art thou called, Odysseus,
By Molü hast thou respite for a little,
By Molü art thou freed from the one bed
    that thou may'st return to another
The stars are not in her counting,
    To her they are but wandering holes.
Begin thy plowing
When the Pleiades go down to their rest,
Begin thy plowing
40 days are they under seabord,
Thus do in fields by seabord
And in valleys winding down toward the sea.
When the cranes fly high
    think of plowing.
By this gate art thou measured
Thy day is between a door and a door
Two oxen are yoked for plowing
Or six in the hill field

White bulk under olives, a score for drawing down stone,
Here the mules are gabled with slate on the hill road.
Thus was it in time.
And the small stars now fall from the olive branch,
Forked shadow falls dark on the terrace
More black than the floating martin
      that has no care for your presence,
His wing-print is black on the roof tiles
And the print is gone with his cry.
So light is thy weight on Tellus
Thy notch no deeper indented
Thy weight less than the shadow
Yet hast thou gnawed through the mountain,
      Scilla's white teeth less sharp.
Hast thou found a nest softer than cunnus
Or hast thou found better rest
Hast'ou a deeper planting, doth thy death year
Bring swifter shoot?
Hast thou entered more deeply the mountain?

The light has entered the cave. Io! Io!
The light has gone down into the cave,
Splendour on splendour!
By prong have I entered these hills:
That the grass grow from my body,
That I hear the roots speaking together,
The air is new on my leaf,
The forked boughs shake with the wind.
Is Zephyrus more light on the bough, Apeliota
more light on the almond branch?
By this door have I entered the hill.

Falleth,
Adonis falleth.
Fruit cometh after. The small lights drift out with the
                                        tide,
sea's claw has gathered them outward,
Four banners to every flower
The sea's claw draws the lamps outward.
Think thus of thy plowing
When the seven stars go down to their rest
Forty days for their rest, by seabord
And in valleys that wind down toward the sea

καὶ Μοῖρα τ᾽ "Αδονιν
KAI MOIRA T᾽ ADONIN

When the almond bough puts forth its flame,
When the new shoots are brought to the altar,

τυ Διῶνα, καὶ Μοῖρα
TU DIONA, KAI MOIRA

καὶ Μοῖρα τ᾽ "Αδονιν
KAI MOIRA T᾽ ADONIN

that hath the gift of healing,
that hath the power over wild beasts.

XLIX

For the seven lakes, and by no man these verses:
Rain; empty river; a voyage,
Fire from frozen cloud, heavy rain in the twilight
Under the cabin roof was one lantern.
The reeds are heavy; bent;
and the bamboos speak as if weeping.

Autumn moon; hills rise about lakes
against sunset
Evening is like a curtain of cloud,
a blurr above ripples; and through it
sharp long spikes of the cinnamon,
a cold tune amid reeds.
Behind hill the monk's bell
borne on the wind.
Sail passed here in April; may return in October
Boat fades in silver; slowly;
Sun blaze alone on the river.

Where wine flag catches the sunset
Sparse chimneys smoke in the cross light

Comes then snow scur on the river
And a world is covered with jade
Small boat floats like a lanthorn,
The flowing water clots as with cold. And at San Yin
they are a people of leisure.
Wild geese swoop to the sand-bar,
Clouds gather about the hole of the window
Broad water; geese line out with the autumn
Rooks clatter over the fishermen's lanthorns,
A light moves on the north sky line;
where the young boys prod stones for shrimp.
In seventeen hundred came Tsing to these hill lakes.
A light moves on the south sky line.

State by creating riches shd. thereby get into debt?
This is infamy; this is Geryon.

This canal goes still to TenShi
though the old king built it for pleasure

KEI	MEN	RAN	KEI
KIU	MAN	MAN	KEI
JITSU	GETSU	KO	KWA
TAN	FUKU	TAN	KAI

Sun up; work
sundown; to rest
dig well and drink of the water
dig field; eat of the grain
Imperial power is? and to us what is it?

The fourth; the dimension of stillness
And the power over wild beasts.

EDITH SITWELL

FROM GOLD COAST CUSTOMS

II

Against the Sea-wall are painted signs
'Here for a shilling a sailor dines.'
Each Rag-and-Bone
Is propped up tall
(Lest in death it fall)
Against the Sea-wall.
Their empty mouths are sewed up whole
Lest from hunger they gape and cough up their sou
The arms of one are stretched out wide...
How long, since our Christ was crucified?

Rich man Judas,
Brother Cain,
The rich men are your worms that gain
The air through seething from your brain;
Judas, mouldering in your old
Coffin body, still undying
As the Worm, where you are lying
With no flesh for warmth, but gold
For flesh, for warmth, for sheet,

Now you are fleshless, too, as these
That starve and freeze,
Is your gold hard as Hell's huge polar street,
Is the universal blackness of Hell's day so cold?

*

When, creeping over
The Sailor's street
Where the houses like ratskin
Masks flap, meet
Never across the murdered bone
Of the sailor, the whining overtone
Of dawn sounds, slaves
Rise from their graves,
Where in the corpse-sheet night they lay
Forgetting the mutilating day,
Like the unborn child in its innocent sleep,
Ah Christ, the murdered light must weep—
(Christ that takest away the sin
Of the world, and the rich man's bone-dead grin)
The light must weep
Seeing that sleep
And those slaves rise up in their death-chains, part
The light from the eyes
The hands from the heart,
Since their hearts are flesh for the tall
And sprawling
Reeling apalling
Cannibal mart,

But their hands and head
Are machines to breed
Gold for the old and the greedy Dead.

I have seen the murdered God look through the eyes
Of the drunkard's smirched
Mask as he lurched
O'er the half of my heart that lies in the street
Neath the dancing fleas and the foul news-sheet.

*

Perhaps if I too lie down in the mud,
Beneath tumbrils rolling
And mad skulls galloping
For from their bunches of nerves that dance
And caper among these slums and prance,
Beneath the noise of that hell that rolls
I shall forget the shrunken souls
The eyeless mud squealing 'God is dead',
Starved men (bags of wind), and the harlot's tread,
The heaven turned into monkey-hide
By Lady Bamburgher's dancing fleas,
Her rotting parties and death-slack ease,
And the dead men drunken
(The only tide)
Blown up and down
And tossed through the town
Over the half of my heart that lies,
Deep down, in this meaner Death with cries.

The leaves of black hippopotamus-hide
Black as the mud
Cover the blood
And the rotting world. Do we smell and see
That sick thick smoke from London burning,
Gomorrah turning
Like worms in the grave,
The Bedlam daylight's murderous roar,
Those pillars of fire the drunkard and whore,
Dirty souls boiled in cannibal cookshops to paper
To make into newspapers, flags? . . . They caper
Like gaping apes. Foul fires we see,
For Bedlam awakes to reality.
The drunken burning,
The skin drums galloping,
In their long march still parched for the sky,
The Rotten Alleys where beggars groan
And the beggar and his dog share a bone;
The rich man Cain that hides within
His lumbering palaces where Sin
Through the eyeless holes of Day peers in,
The murdered heart that all night turns
From small machine to shapeless Worm
With hate, and like Gomorrah burns—
These put the eyes of Heaven out,
These raise all Hell's throats to a shout,
These break my heart's walls toppling in,
And like a universal sea
The nations of the Dead crowd in.

*

Gomorrah's fires have washed my blood—
But the fires of God shall wash the mud
Till the skin drums rolling
The slum cries sprawling
And crawling
Are calling
'Burn thou me!'
Though Death has taken
And pig-like shaken
Rooted and tossed
The rags of me.
Yet the time will come
To the heart's dark slum
When the rich man's gold and the rich man's wheat
Will grow in the street, that the starved may eat,—
And the sea of the rich will give up its dead—
And the last blood and fire from my side will be shed.
For the fires of God go marching on.

EARLY SPRING

The wooden châlets of the cloud
Hang down their dull blunt ropes to shroud

Red crystal bells upon each bough
(Fruit-buds that whimper). No winds slough

Our faces, furred with cold like red
Furred buds of satyr springs, long dead!

The cold wind creaking in my blood
Seems part of it, as grain of wood;

Among the coarse goat-locks of snow
Mamzelle still drags me to and fro;

Her feet make marks like centaur hoofs
In hairy snow; her cold reproofs

Die, and her strange eyes look oblique
As the slant crystal buds that creak.

If she could think me distant, she
In the snow's goat-locks certainly

Would try to milk those teats, the buds,
Of their warm sticky milk—the cuds

Of strange long-past fruit-hairy springs—
Beginnings of first earthy things!

AUBADE

Jane, Jane,
Tall as a crane,
The morning light creaks down again.

Comb your cockscomb-ragged hair,
Jane, Jane, come down the stair.

Each dull blunt wooden stalactite
Of rain creaks, hardened by the light,

Sounding like an overtone
From some lonely world unknown.

But the creaking empty light
Will never harden into sight,

Will never penetrate your brain
With overtones like the blunt rain.

The light would show (if it could harden)
Eternities of kitchen garden,

Cockscomb flowers that none will pluck,
And wooden flowers that 'gin to cluck.

In the kitchen you must light
Flames as staring, red and white,

As carrots or as turnips, shining
Where the cold dawn light lies whining.

Cockscomb hair on the cold wind
Hangs limp, turns the milk's weak mind....
          Jane, Jane,
          Tall as a crane,
          The morning light creaks down again!

ROMANCE

For Rée Gorer

She grew within his heart as the flushed rose
In the green heat of the long summer grows
Deep in the sorrowful heaven of her leaves.
And this song only is the sound that grieves
When the gold-fingered wind from the green veins
Of the rich rose deflowers her amber blood,
The sharp green rains.
Such is the song, grown from a sleepy head,
Of lovers in a country paradise.
You shall not find it where a song-bird flies,
Nor from the sound that in a bird-throat grieves,
Its chart lies not in maps on strawberry leaves.

Green were the pomp and pleasure of the shade
Wherein they dwelt; like country temples green
The huge leaves bear a dark-mosaic'd sheen
Like gold on forest temples richly laid.

And swan-skin leaves of cherries seem a cloud
Where coral tears of the rich light fall loud
In that smooth darkness; the gourds dark as caves
Hold thick gold honey for their fountain waves,

Figs dark and wrinkled as Silenus hold
Rubies and garnets, and the melons cold
Waves like a fountain; falling on the grass
The apples boom like sharp green summer rain.

But Time drifts by as the long-plumaged winds
And the dark swans whose plumes seem weeping leaves
In the shade's deepest splendour—these drift by.
And sometimes he would turn to her and sigh:

'The bright swans leave the wave... so leave not me.
With Aethiopǣa, smooth Aëropē
Amid the pomp and splendour of the shade
Their rich and leafy plumes a lulling music made.

Dark are their plumes, and dark the airs that grew
Amid those weeping leaves.
Plantations of the East drop precious dew
That ripened by the light, rich leaves perspire,
Such are the drops that from the bright swans' feathers
                                                flew.

Come then, my pomp and pleasure of the shade,
Most lovely cloud that the hot sun made black
As dark-leaved swans.
                        Come then, O precious cloud,
Lean to my heart. No shade of some rich tree
Shall pour such splendour as your heart to me.'

So these two lovers dreamed the time away
Beside smooth waters like the honey waves
In the ripe melons that are dark as caves;
Eternity seemed but a summer day.

And they forgot, seeing the Asian train
Of waves upon the glittering wide sea main

And rich gold waves from fountain caverns run,
That all the splendour of the eastern sun,

And many a rose-shaped heart must lie beneath
The maps on strawberry leaves dark green as snows,
With amber dust that was a nymph or rose—

And worlds more vast lie ruined by sad Time
That is the conqueror of our green clime.

For even the beasts eschew the shrunken heart
That dieth of itself, small deaths devour—
Or that worm mightier than death's—the small corroding
                                        hour.

How ancient is the Worm, companionless
As the black dust of Venus? Dulled to this
And loathèd as the Worm, she is alone
Though all the morbid suns lay in her kiss.

How old, the small undying snake that wreathes
Round lips and eyes, now that the kiss has gone?
In that last night, when we, too, are alone
We have, for love that seemed eternity
The old unchanging memory of the bone—
That porphyry whence grew the summer rose.

Most ancient is the Worm—more old than night
Or the first music heard among the trees
And the unknown horizons' harmonies

Where the huge suns come freshened. Shrunk and cold
Is he, like Venus blackened, noseless, old.

Yet all immensities lie in his strong
Embrace, horizons that no sight hath known,
The veins whose sea had heard the siren song
And worlds that grew from an immortal kiss.

And still their love amid this green world grieves,
'The gold light drips like myrrh upon the leaves
And fills with gold those chambers of the South
That were your eyes, that honeycomb your mouth.

And now the undying Worm makes no great stir,
His tight embrace chills not our luxuries
Though the last light perfumes our bones like myrrh
And Time's beat dies.
                            Come, with your kiss renew
The day till all the old worlds die like dew.

When the green century of summer rains
Lay on the leaves, then like the rose I wept.
For I had dwelt in sorrow as the rose
In the deep heaven of her leaves lies close.
Then you, my gardener, with green fingers stroked my
                                                    leaves
Till all the gold drops turned to honey. Grieves
This empire of green shade when honeyed rains
And amber blood flush all the sharp green veins
Of the rich rose?
                            So doth my rose-shaped heart

Feel the first flush of summer; love's first smart
Seemed no more sorrowful than the deep tears
The rose wept in that green and honeyed clime.

The green rains drip like the slow beat of Time
That grows within the amber blood, green veins
Of the rich rose, and in the rose-shaped heart—
Changing the amber flesh to a clay wall.
Then comes the endless cold
At last, that is the Zero, mighty, old,
Huge as the heart, but than the worm more small—
Our final structure, the heart's ragged dress
That rose from Nothing, fell to Nothingness.

For the vast universal Night shall cover
The earth from Pole to Pole, and like a lover
Invade your heart that changed into my stone,
And I your Sisyphus. We two shall lie
Like those within the grave's eternity
And dream our arms hold the horizons deep
Where the strong suns come freshened from deep seas,
The continents beyond discoveries,
Eternal youth, and the god's wisdom, sleep.

How should I dream that I must wake alone
With a void coffin of sad flesh and bone—
You, with the small undying serpent's kiss,
You, the dull rumour of the dust's renown—
The polar night, a boulder rolling down
My heart, your Sisyphus, to that abyss

Where is nor light, nor dark, nor soul, nor heart to eat—
Only the dust of all the dead, the sound of passing feet.'

So winter fell, the heart shaped like the rose
Beneath the mountain of oblivion lies
With all death's nations and the centuries.
And this song ending fades like the shrill snows,

Dim as the languid moon's vast fading light
That scatters sparkles faint and dim and chill
Upon the wide leaves round my window-sill
Like Aethiopaea ever jewelled bright . . .

So fading from the branches the snow sang
With a strange perfume, a melodious twang
As if a rose should change into a ghost—
A ghost turn to a perfume on the leaves.

LULLABY

Though the world has slipped and gone,
Sounds my loud discordant cry
Like the steel birds' song on high:
"Still one thing is left—the Bone."
Then out danced the Babioun.

She sat in the hollow of the sea—
A socket whence the eye's put out—
She sang to the child a lullaby
(The steel birds' nest was thereabout).

Note.—The phrase "out-dance the Babioun" occurs in an Epigram by Ben Jonson.

"Do, do, do, do—
Thy mother's hied to the vaster race:
The Pterodactyl made its nest
And laid a steel egg in her breast—
Under the Judas-coloured sun.
She'll work no more, nor dance, nor moan,
And I am come to take her place
Do—do.

There's nothing left but earth's low bed—
(The Pterodactyl fouls its nest):
But steel wings fan thee to thy rest,
And wingless truth and larvae lie
And eyeless hope and handless fear—
All these for thee as toys are spread,
Do, do.

Red is the bed of Poland, Spain,
And thy mother's breast, who has grown wise
In that fouled nest. If she could rise,
Give birth again,

In wolfish pelt she'd hide thy bones
To shield thee from the world's long cold,
And down on all fours shouldst thou crawl
For thus from no height canst thou fall—
Do, do.

She'd give no hands: there's nought to hold
And nought to make: there's dust to sift,
But no food for the hands to lift.
Do, do.

Heed my ragged lullaby,
Fear not living, fear not chance;
All is equal—blindness, sight,
There is no depth, there is no height:
Do, do,

The Judas-coloured sun is gone,
And with the Ape thou art alone—
Do,
        Do."

STREET SONG

"Love my heart for an hour, but my bone for a day—
At least the skeleton smiles, for it has a morrow:
But the hearts of the young are now the dark treasure
                                of Death,
And summer is lonely.

Comfort the lonely light and the sun in its sorrow,
Come like the night, for terrible is the sun
As truth, and the dying light shows only the
                                skeleton's hunger
For peace, under the flesh like the summer rose.

Come through the darkness of death, as once through
                                the branches
Of youth you came, through the shade like the
                                flowering door
That leads into Paradise, far from the street,—you,
                                the unborn
City seen by the homeless, the night of the poor.

You walk in the city ways, where Man's threatening
shadow
Red-edged by the sun like Cain, has a changing shape—
Elegant like the Skeleton, crouched like the Tiger,
With the age-old wisdom and aptness of the Ape.

The pulse that beats in the heart is changed to the hammer
That sounds in the Potter's Field where they build
a new world
From our Bone, and the carrion-bird days' foul droppings
and clamour—
But you are my night, and my peace,—

The holy night of conception, of rest, the consoling
Darkness when all men are equal,—the wrong
and the right,
And the rich and the poor are no longer separate
nations,—
They are brothers in night."

This was the song I heard; but the Bone is silent!
Who knows if the sound was that of the dead light
calling,—
Of Caesar rolling onward his heart, that stone,
Or the burden of Atlas falling.

TATTERED SERENADE: BEGGAR TO SHADOW

To Robert Herring

> ("*Je m'en allais, les poings dans mes poches crevées;*
> *Mon paletot aussi devenait idéal;*
> *J'allais sous le ciel, Muse, et j'étais ton féal.*
> *Oh là là, que d'amours splendides j'ai rêvées."*
>
> Arthur Rimbaud)

I

These are the nations of the Dead, their million-year-old
Rags about them,—these, the eternally cold,
Misery's worlds, with Hunger, their long sun
Shut in by polar worlds of ice, known to no other,
Without a name, without a brother,
Though their skin shows that they yet are men,

Airing their skeletons' well-planned cities where,
Left by the rose, the flesh, with truth alone,
The fevers of the world and of the heart,
The light of the sun, are gone.

And to their only friend, the Shade
They cast, their muttering voices sing this Serenade:

"O Shade! Gigantic and adaptable Ape,
With the elegance of the skeleton
In your black tattered cape—
How like, and yet how unlike, you are to our last state!

You, too, have giant hands,—but have no thumbs
In a world where nothing is to make or hold,
Nor have you that appalling gulf the hearth,—
Or that red gulf the gullet where only Hunger comes.

For face, you have a hollow wolf-grey cowl
Like mine ... no voice to howl—

(O plain of winter wolves beneath my hearth!)
And no identity! No face to weep!
No bed—unlike the rich men who can creep
Into the pocks made by that vast disease
That is our civilisation, once there, lie at ease!

No memory,—no years,
Nothing to feel or think,
No friend from whom to part with youthful tears.
But your unutterable tatters cannot stink!

My overcoat, like yours, is an Ideal,
With a gulf for pockets—nothing there to steal
But my empty hands, that long have lost their use,
With nothing now to make, or hold, or lose.

Yet when spring comes, a world is in my head,
And dreams, for those who never have a bed—

The thought of a day when all may be possible,—all
May come my way," said small Rag-Castle to Rag-
Castle tall,—

The young, that have no covering between
Their outer tatters and the worthless skin
That shows the air, the rain, they yet are men,

When remembering it is spring, falls the warm rain
Like lilies of the vale,
Buds golden-pale
Sprouting from pavements, on a universe of coins,
endless gold

Pelting the homeless, who have no dress
Against the winter cold,
But the skeleton, that burgh of idleness
Where only the worm works . . . those that are alone
Except for hunger, thirst, and lust;
For the fevers of the world and of the heart,
The summer rose, are gone.

II

In the summer, when noone is cold,
And the country roads seem of hot gold,

While the air seems a draught of white wine
Where all day long golden stars shine,—

And the sun is a world of red meat
For those who have nothing to eat,

I walk the world, envying the roads
That have somewhere to go, that bear loads

Of happiness, business, and sorrow,
And the rose that cares not for tomorrow;

But I've nothing to hold or to lose,
And my hands have long since lost their use;

While my overcoat's but an Ideal,—
In my pockets there's nothing to steal.

But the roads have north, east, west, and south,
For their food, though I've none for my mouth

Or my empty red gulf of a heart—
I have no friend from whom I must part

But the shade that I cast,—my one friend
Till at last the world comes to an end.

His face is a wolfish grey cowl
Like my own, but without the wolf's howl,

For like me, he's a face, but no tears
He can shed, neither memory nor years.

But the Shadow has never known cold,
And the Shadow will never grow old,—

The black tatters he wears cannot stink
And he neither can feel, fear, or think,

While a universe grows in my head,—
I have dreams, though I have not a bed—

The thought of a world and a day
When all may be possible, still come my way

As I walk the long roads of hot gold
In the summer, when noone is cold.

HEART AND MIND

Said the Lion to the Lioness—'When you are amber
dust,—
No more a raging fire like the heat of the Sun
(No liking but all lust)—
Remember still the flowering of the amber blood and
bone
The rippling of bright muscles like a sea,
Remember the rose-prickles of bright paws
Though we shall mate no more
Till the fire of that sun the heart and the moon-cold bone
are one.'

Said the Skeleton lying upon the sands of Time—
'The great gold planet that is the mourning heat of the Sun
Is greater than all gold, more powerful
Than the tawny body of a Lion that fire consumes
Like all that grows or leaps . . . so is the heart
More powerful than all dust. Once I was Hercules
Or Samson, strong as the pillars of the seas:
But the flames of the heart consumed me, and the mind
Is but a foolish wind.'

Said the Sun to the Moon—'When you are but a lonely
                                        white crone,
And I, a dead King in my golden armour somewhere
                                        in a dark wood,
Remember only this of our hopeless love
That never till Time is done
Will the fire of the heart and the fire of the mind be one.'

INVOCATION

For Alec and Merula Guinness

I who was once a golden woman like those who walk
In the dark heavens—but am now grown old
And sit by the fire, and see the fire grow cold,
Watch the dark fields for a rebirth of faith and of
                                        wonder.

The turning of Ixion's wheel the day
Ceased not, yet sounds no more the beat of the heart
But only the sound of ultimate Darkness falling
And of the Blind Samson at the Fair, shaking the pillars
                                of the world and emptily calling.

For the gardeners cried for rain, but the high priests
                                        howled
For a darker rain to cool the delirium of gold
And wash the sore of the world, the heart of Dives,
Raise wheat for the hunger that lies in the soul of
                                        the poor—
Then came the thunderous darkness

And the fly-like whispering of small hopes, small fears,
The gossips of mean Death—gadflies and gnats,
                    the summer world:
The small and gilded scholars of the Fly
That feed upon the crowds and their dead breath
And buzz and stink where the bright heroes die
Of the dust's rumours and the old world's fevers.
Then fell the world in winter.

But I, a golden woman like the corn goddess
Watch the dark fields, and know when spring begins
To the sound of the heart and the planetary rhythm,
Fires in the heavens and in the hearts of men,
Young people and young flowers come out in the
                    darkness.

And where are they going? How should I know? I
                    see only
The hierarchies love the young people—the Swan has
                    given his snows
And Berenice her wild mane to make their fair hair,
And speaking of love are the voices that come from the
                    darkness:

Of the nobler love of Man for his brother Man,
And of how the creeds of the world shall no more divide
                    them
But every life be that of a country Fate
Whose wheel had a golden woof and warp, the Day—
Woven of threads of the common task; and light
Tells to that little child the humble dust

Tales of the old world's holiness, finds veins of ore
In the unripe wheat-ear; and the common fire
That drops with seed like the Sun's, is fallen from the
long-leaved planets.

So when the winter of the world and Man's fresh Fall
When democratic Death feared no more the heart's
coldness
Shall be forgotten,
O Love, return to the dying world, as the light
Of morning, shining in all regions, latitudes
And households of high heaven within the heart.

Be then our visible world, our world invisible!
Throughout our day like the laughing flames of the Sun
Lie on our leaves of life, your heat infusing
Deep in the amber blood of the smooth tree.
The panic splendour of the animal
Is yours — O primal Law
That rules the blood (the solar ray in the veins)—
The fire of the hearth, the household Deity
That shines not, nor does it burn, destroy like fire,
But nourishes with its endless wandering
Like that of the Golden Ones in the high heavens.

Rule then the spirit working in dark earth
As the Sun and Planets rule the husbandman–
O pride that in each semitone
Of amber blood and bone
Proclaims the splendour that arose from the first Dark!

Be too the ear of wheat to the Lost Men
Who ask the city stones if they are bread
And the stones of the city weep....

                         You, the lost days
When all might still be hoped for, and the light
Laid gold in the unhopeful path of the poor—
The shrunken darkness in the miser's heart.

Now falls the night of the world:—O Spirit moving upon
                      the waters
Your peace instil
In the animal heat and splendour of the blood—
The hot gold of the sun that flames in the night
And knows not down-going
But moves with the revolutions in the heavens.

The thunders and the fires and acclamations
Of the leaves of spring are stilled, but in the night
The Holy Ghost speaks in the whispering leaves.
O wheat-ear shining like a fire and the bright gold,
O water brought from far to the dying gardens!

Bring peace to the famine of the heart and lips,
And to the Last Man's loneliness
Of those who dream they can bring back sight to
                    the blind!
You are the Night
When the long hunt for Nothing is at rest
In the Blind Man's Street, and in the human breast

The hammer of Chaos is stilled.
                             Be then the sleep
When Judas gives again the childish kiss
That once his mother knew—and wash the stain
From the darkened hands of the universal Cain.

W. H. AUDEN

CHORUSES

from Paid on Both Sides

I

Can speak of trouble, pressure on men
Born all the time, brought forward into light
For warm dark moan.
Though heart fears all heart cries for, rebuffs
                    with mortal beat
Skyfall, the legs sucked under, adder's bite.
That prize held out of reach
Guides the unwilling tread,
The asking breath,
Till on attended bed
Or in untracked dishonour comes to each
His natural death.

We pass our days
Speak, man to men, easy, learning to point
To jump before ladies, to show our scars:
But no
We were mistaken, these faces are not ours.
They smile no more when we smile back:

Eyes, ears, tongue, nostrils bring
News of revolt, inadequate counsel to
An infirm king.

O watcher in the dark, you wake
Our dream of waking, we feel
Your finger on the flesh that has been skinned,
By your bright day
See clear what we were doing, that we were vile.
Your sudden hand
Shall humble great
Pride, break it, wear down to stumps old
                              systems which await
The last transgression of the sea.

II

The Spring unsettles sleeping partnerships,
Foundries improve their casting process, shops
Open a further wing on credit till
The winter. In summer boys grow tall
With running races on the froth-wet sand,
War is declared there, here a treaty signed;
Here a scrum breaks up like a bomb, there troops
Deploy like birds. But proudest into traps
Have fallen. These gears which ran in oil for
                                  week
By week, needing no look, now will not work;
Those manors mortgaged twice to pay for love
Go to another.

O how shall man live
Whose thought is born, child of one farcical
night,
To find him old? The body warm but not
By choice, he dreams of folk in dancing bunches,
Of tart wine spilt on home-made benches,
Where learns, one drawn apart, a secret will
Restore the dead; but comes thence to a wall.
Outside on frozen soil lie armies killed
Who seem familiar but they are cold.
Now the most solid wish he tries to keep
His hands show through; he never will look up,
Say 'I am good'. On him misfortune falls
More than enough. Better where no one feels,
The out-of-sight, buried too deep for shafts.

III

Though he believe it, no man is strong.
He thinks to be called the fortunate,
To bring home a wife, to live long.

But he is defeated; let the son
Sell the farm lest the mountain fall;
His mother and her mother won.

His fields are used up where th moles visit,
The contours worn flat; if there show
Passage for water he will miss it:

Give up his breath, his woman, his team;
No life to touch, though later there be
Big fruit, eagles above the stream.

"DOOM IS DARK"

Doom is dark and deeper than any sea-dingle.
Upon what man it fall
In spring, day-wishing flowers appearing,
Avalanche sliding, white snow from rock-face,
That he should leave his house,
No cloud-soft hand can hold him, restraint by women;
But ever that man goes
Through place-keepers, through forest trees,
A stranger to strangers over undried sea,
Houses for fishes, suffocating water,
Or lonely on fell as chat,
By pot-holed becks
A bird stone-haunting, an unquiet bird.

There head falls forward, fatigued at evening,
And dreams of home,
Waving from window, spread of welcome,
Kissing of wife under single sheet;
But waking sees
Bird-flocks nameless to him, through doorway voices
Of new men making another love.

Save him from hostile capture,
From sudden tiger's spring at corner;

Protect his house,
His anxious house where days are counted
From thunderbolt protect,
From gradual ruin spreading like a stain;
Converting number from vague to certain,
Bring joy, bring day of his returning,
Lucky with day approaching, with leaning dawn.

"ITS NO USE"

Its no use raising a shout.
No, Honey, you can cut that right out.
I don't want any more hugs;
Make me some fresh tea, fetch me some rugs.
Here am I, here are you:
But what does it mean? What are we going to do?

A long time ago I told my mother
I was leaving home to find another:
I never answered her letter
But I never found a better.
Here am I, here are you:
But what does it mean? What are we going to do?

It wasn't always like this?
Perhaps it wasn't, but it is.
Put the car away; when life fails,
What's the good of going to Wales?
Here am I, here are you:
But what does it mean? What are we going to do?

In my spine there was a base;
And I knew the general's face:
But they've severed all the wires,
And I can't tell what the general desires.
Here am I, here are you:
But what does it mean? What are we going to do?

In my veins there is a wish,
And a memory of fish:
When I lie crying on the floor,
It says, 'You've often done this before.'
Here am I, here are you:
But what does it mean? What are we going to do?

A bird used to visit this shore:
It isn't going to come any more.
I've come a very long way to prove
No land, no water, and no love.
Here am I, here are you:
But what does it mean? What are we going to do?

"IT IS TIME"

It is time for the destruction of error.
The chairs are being brought in from the garden,
The summer talk stopped on that savage coast
Before the storms, after the guests and birds:
In sanatoriums they laugh less and less,
Less certain of cure; and the loud madman
Sinks now into a more terrible calm.

The falling leaves know it, the children,
At play on the fuming alkali-tip
Or by the flooded football ground, know it—
This is the dragon's day, the devourer's:
Orders are given to the enemy for a time
With underground proliferation of mould,
With constant whisper and the casual question,
To haunt the poisoned in his shunned house,
To destroy the efflorescence of the flesh,
The intricate play of the mind, to enforce
Conformity with the orthodox bone,
With organized fear, the articulated skeleton.

You whom I gladly walk with, touch,
Or wait for as one certain of good,
We know it, we know that love
Needs more than the admiring excitement of union,
More than the abrupt self-confident farewell,
The heel on the finishing blade of grass,
The self-confidence of the falling root,
Needs death, death of the grain, our death,
Death of the old gang; would leave them
In sullen valley where is made no friend,
The old gang to be forgotten in the spring,
The hard bitch and the riding-master,
Stiff underground; deep in clear lake
The lolling bridegroom, beautiful, there.

"ON SUNDAY WALKS"

On Sunday walks
Past the shut gates of works
The conquerors come
And are handsome.

Sitting all day
By the open window
Say what they say
Know what to know
Who brought and taught
Unusual images
And new tunes to old cottages,
With so much done
Without a thought
Of the anonymous lampoon
The cellar counterplot,
Though in the night
Pursued by eaters
They clutch at gaiters
That straddle and deny
Escape that way,
Though in the night
Is waking fright.

Father by son
Lives on and on
Though over date
And motto on the gate
The lichen grows

From year to year,
Still here and there
That Roman nose
Is noticed in the villages
And father's son
Knows what they said
And what they did.

Not meaning to deceive,
Wish to give suck
Enforces make-believe
And what was fear
Of fever and bad-luck
Is now a scare
At certain names
A need for charms
For certain words
At certain fords
And what was livelihood
Is tallness, strongness
Words and longness,
All glory and all story
Solemn and not so good.

"TALLER TO-DAY, WE REMEMBER"

Taller to-day, we remember similar evenings,
Walking together in the windless orchard
Where the brook runs over the gravel, far from the
           glacier.

Again in the room with the sofa hiding the grate,
Look down to the river when the rain is over,
See him turn to the window, hearing our last
Of Captain Ferguson.

It is seen how excellent hands have turned to commonness.
One staring too long, went blind in a tower,
One sold all his manors to fight, broke through, and
                                                    faltered.

Nights come bringing the snow, and the dead howl
Under the headlands in their windy dwelling
Because the Adversary put too easy questions
On lonely roads.

But happy now, though no nearer each other,
We see the farms lighted all along the valley;
Down at the mill-shed the hammering stops
And men go home.

Noises at dawn will bring
Freedom for some, but not this peace
No bird can contradict: passing, but is sufficient now
For something fulfilled this hour, loved or endured.

"CONSIDER THIS"

Consider this and in our time
As the hawk sees it or the helmeted airman:
The clouds rift suddenly—look there
At cigarette-end smouldering on a border

At the first garden party of the year.
Pass on, admire the view of the massif
Through plate-glass windows of the Sport Hotel;
Join there the insufficient units
Dangerous, easy, in furs, in uniform
And constellated at reserved tables
Supplied with feelings by an efficient band
Relayed elsewhere to farmers and their dogs
Sitting in kitchens in the stormy fens.

Long ago, supreme Antagonist,
More powerful than the great northern whale
Ancient and sorry at life's limiting defect,
In Cornwall, Mendip, or the Pennine moor
Your comments on the highborn mining-captains,
Found they no answer, made them wish to die
——Lie since in barrows out of harm
You talk to your admirers every day
By silted harbours, derelict works,
In strangled orchards, and the silent comb
Where dogs have worried or a bird was shot.
Order the ill that they attack at once:
Visit the ports and, interrupting
The leisurely conversation in the bar
Within a stone's throw of the sunlit water,
Beckon your chosen out. Summon
Those handsome and diseased youngsters, those women
Your solitary agents in the country parishes;
And mobilize the powerful forces latent
In soils that make the farmer brutal
In the infected sinus, and the eyes of stoats.

Then, ready, start your rumour, soft
But horrifying in its capacity to disgust
Which, spreading magnified, shall come to be
A polar peril, a prodigious alarm,
Scattering the people, as torn-up paper
Rags and utensils in a sudden gust,
Seized with immeasurable neurotic dread.

Financier, leaving your little room
Where the money is made but not spent,
You'll need your typist and your boy no more;
The game is up for you and for the others,
Who, thinking, pace in slippers on the lawns
Of College Quad or Cathedral Close,
Who are born nurses, who live in shorts
Sleeping with people and playing fives.
Seekers after happiness, all who follow
The convolutions of your simple wish,
It is later than you think; nearer that day
Far other than that distant afternoon
Amid rustle of frocks and stamping feet
They gave the prizes to the ruined boys.
You cannot be away, then, no
Not though you pack to leave within an hour,
Escaping humming down arterial roads:
The date was yours; the prey to fugues,
Irregular breathing and alternate ascendancies
After some haunted migratory years
To disintegrate on an instans in the explosion of mania
Or lapse for ever into a classic fatigue.

"SIR, NO MAN'S ENEMY"

Sir, no man's enemy, forgiving all
But will his negative inversion, be prodigal:
Send to us power and light, a sovereign touch
Curing the intolerable neural itch,
The exhaustion of weaning, the liar's quinsy,
And the distortions of ingrown virginity.
Prohibit sharply the rehearsed response
And gradually correct the coward's stance;
Cover in time with beams those in retreat
That, spotted, they turn though the reverse were great;
Publish each healer that in city lives
Or country houses at the end of drives;
Harrow the house of the dead; look shining at
New styles of architecture, a change of heart.

"WATCHING IN THREE PLANES"

Watching in three planes from a room overlooking the
                               courtyard
              That year decaying,
Stub-end of year that smoulders to ash of winter,
              The last day dropping;
Lo, a dream met me in middle night, I saw in a vision
Life pass as a gull, as a spy, as a dog-hated dustman:
Heard a voice saying—'Wystan, Stephen, Christopher,
                            all of you,
            Read of your losses'.

Shaped me a Lent scene first, a bed, hard, surgical,
          And a wound hurting;
The hour in the night when Lawrence died and I came
          Round from the morphia.
A train went clanking over the bridges leaving the city;
A sleep-walker pushed on groaning down the velvet
          passage;
The night-nurse visited—'We shall not all sleep, dearie',
          She said, and left me.

Felt sap collecting anon in unlighted cylinders
          For birdward facing;
The flat snake moving again in the pit, the schoolboy
          From home migrating.
After a night of storm was a lawn in sunlight,
A colleague bending for measurements there at the rain-
          gauge,
Gritting his teeth after breakfast, the Headmaster
          muttered
          'Call no man happy'.

Came summer like a flood, did never greediest gardener
          Make blossoms flusher:
Sunday meant lakes for many, a browner body
          Beauty from burning:
Far out in the water two heads discussed the position,
Out of the reeds like a fowl jumped the undressed
          German,
And Stephen signalled from the sand dunes like a wooden
          madman
          'Destroy this temple'.

It did fall. The quick hare died to the hound's hot
                                        breathing,
                    The Jewess fled Southwards;
The drunken Scotsman, regarding the moons hedgerising,
              Shook and saluted:
And in cold Europe, in the middle of Autumn destruc-
                            tion,
Christopher stood, his face grown lined with wincing
In front of ignorance—'Tell the English', he shivered,
                    'Man is a spirit'.

What I saw further was general but in sorrow,
                    Many together
Forgiving each other in the dark of the picture palaces
                    But past forgiveness;
The pair walking out on the mole, getting ready to
                                        quarrel,
The exile from superb Africa, employed in a laundry;
Deserters, mechanics, conjurers, delicate martyrs,
                    Yes, self-regarders.

I saw the brain-track perfected, laid for conveying
                    The fatal error,
Sending the body to islands or after its father,
              Cold with a razor:
One sniffed at a root to make him dream of a woman,
One laid his hands on the heads of dear little pages;
Neither in the bed nor on the *arrête* was there shown me
                    One with power.

'Save me!' the voice commanded, but as I paused
                                            hesitant
            A troop rushed forward.
Of all the healers, granny in mittens, the Mop, the white
                                            surgeon,
            And loony Layard.
The captains grouped round the flagstaff shut up their
                                            glasses,
Broke yelping over the gravel—as I stood a spectator;
One tapped my shoulder and asked me 'How did you
                                            fall, sir?'
            Whereat I awakened.

Roof-line sharpens, intense in the New Year morning;
            Far down in courtyard
Beggar addresses the earth on the state of East Europe:
            'Won't you speak louder?
Have you heard of someone swifter than Syrian horses?
Has he thrown the bully of Corinth in the sanded circle?
Has he crossed the Isthmus already? is he seeking brilliant
                                            Athens and us?'

PROLOGUE

O love, the interest itself in thoughtless Heaven,
Make simpler daily the beating of man's heart; within,
There in the ring where name and image meet,

Inspire them with such a longing as will make his thought
Alive like patterns a murmuration of starlings
Rising in joy over wolds unwittingly weave;

Here too on our little reef display your power,
This fortress perched on the edge of the Atlantic scarp,
The mole between all Europe and the exile-crowded sea;

And make us as Newton was, who in his garden matching
The apple falling towards England, became aware
Between himself and her of an eternal tie.

For now that dream which so long has contented our will,
I mean, of uniting the dead into a splendid empire,
Under whose fertilising flood the Lancashire moss

Sprouted up chimneys, and Glamorgan hid a life
Grim as a tidal rock-pool's in its glove-shaped valleys,
Is already retreating into her maternal shadow;

Leaving the furnaces gasping in the impossible air,
The flotsam at which Dumbarton gapes and hungers;
While upon wind-loved Rowley no hammer shakes

The cluster of mounds like a midget golf course, graves
Of some who created these intelligible dangerous marvels;
Affectionate people, but crude their sense of glory.

Far-sighted as falcons, they looked down another future;
For the seed in their loins were hostile, though afraid of
                                        their pride,
And, tall with a shadow now, inertly wait.

In bar, in netted chicken-farm, in lighthouse,
Standing on these impoverished constricting acres,
The ladies and gentlemen apart, too much alone,

Consider the years of the measured world begun,
The barren spiritual marriage of stone and water.
Yet, O, at this very moment of our hopeless sigh

When inland they are thinking their thoughts but are
                                    watching these islands,
As children in Chester look to Moel Fammau to decide
On picnics by the clearness or withdrawal of her treeless
                                    crown,

Some possible dream, long coiled in the ammonite's slum-
                                    ber
Is uncurling, prepared to lay on our talk and kindness
Its military silence, its surgeon's idea of pain;

And out of the Future into actual History,
As when Merlin, tamer of horses, and his lords to whom
Stonehenge was still a thought, the Pillars passed

And into the undared ocean swung north their prow,
Drives through the night and star-concealing dawn
For the virgin roadsteads of our hearts an unwavering
                                    keel.

"HEARING OF HARVESTS"

Hearing of harvests rotting in the valleys,
Seeing at end of street the barren mountains,
Round corners coming suddenly on water,
Knowing them shipwrecked who were launched for
                                    islands,

We honour founders of these starving cities,
Whose honour is the image of our sorrow.

Which cannot see its likeness in their sorrow
That brought them desperate to the brink of valleys;
Dreaming of evening walks through learned cities,
They reined their violent horses on the mountains,
Those fields like ships to castaways on islands,
Visions of green to them that craved for water.

They built by rivers and at night the water
Running past windows comforted their sorrow;
Each in his little bed conceived of islands
Where every day was dancing in the valleys,
And all the year trees blossomed on the mountains,
Where love was innocent, being far from cities.

But dawn came back and they were still in cities;
No marvellous creature rose up from the water,
There was still gold and silver in the mountains,
And hunger was a more immediate sorrow;
Although to moping villagers in valleys
Some waving pilgrims were describing islands.

'The gods', they promised, 'visit us from islands,
Are stalking head-up, lovely through the cities;
Now is the time to leave your wretched valleys
And sail with them across the lime-green water;
Sitting at their white sides, forget their sorrow,
The shadow cast across your lives by mountains.'

So many, doubtful, perished in the mountains
Climbing up crags to get a view of islands;
So many, fearful, took with them their sorrow
Which stayed them when they reached unhappy cities;
So many, careless, dived and drowned in water;
So many, wretched, would not leave their valleys.

It is the sorrow; shall it melt? Ah, water
Would gush, flush, green these mountains and these
                                    valleys,
And we rebuild our cities, not dream of islands.

"FISH IN THE UNRUFFLED LAKES"

Fish in the unruffled lakes
The swarming colours wear,
Swans in the winter air
A white perfection have,
And the great lion walks
Through his innocent grove;
Lion, fish, and swan
Act, and are gone
Upon Time's toppling wave.

We till shadowed days are done,
We must weep and sing
Duty's conscious wrong,
The Devil in the clock,
The Goodness carefully worn
For atonement or for luck;
We must lose our loves,

On each beast and bird that moves
Turn an envious look.

Sighs for folly said and done
Twist our narrow days;
But I must bless, I must praise
That you, my swan, who have
All gifts that to the swan
Impulsive Nature gave,
The majesty and pride,
Last night should add
Your voluntary love.

SPAIN

Yesterday all the past. The language of size
Spreading to China along the trade-routes; the diffusion
        Of the counting-frame and the cromlech;
Yesterday the shadow-reckoning in the sunny climates.

Yesterday the assessment of insurance by cards,
The divination of water; yesterday the invention
        Of cartwheels and clocks, the taming of
Horses. Yesterday the bustling world of the navigators.

Yesterday the abolition of fairies and giants,
The fortress like a motionless eagle eyeing the valley,
        The chapel built in the forest;
Yesterday the carving of angels and alarming gargoyles.

The trial of heretics among the columns of stone;
Yesterday the theological feuds in the taverns
      And the miraculous cure at the fountain;
Yesterday the Sabbath of witches; but to-day the struggle.

Yesterday the installation of dynamos and turbines,
The construction of railways in the colonial desert;
      Yesterday the classic lecture
On the origin of Mankind. But to-day the struggle.

Yesterday the belief in the absolute value of Greece,
The fall of the curtain upon the death of a hero;
      Yesterday the prayer to the sunset
And the adoration of madmen. But to-day the struggle.

As the poet whispers, startled among the pines,
Or where the loose waterfall sings compact, or upright
      On the crag by the leaning tower:
'O my vision. O send me the luck of the sailor.'

And the investigator peers through his instruments
At the inhuman provinces, the virile bacillus
      Or enormous Jupiter finished:
'But the lives of my friends. I inquire. I inquire.'

And the poor in their fireless lodgings, dropping the sheets
Of the evening paper: 'Our day is our loss, O show us
      History the operator, the
Organiser, Time the refreshing river.'

And the nations combine each cry, invoking the life
That shapes the individual belly and orders
        The private nocturnal terror:
'Did you not found the city state of the sponge,

'Raise the vast military empires of the shark
And the tiger, establish the robin's plucky canton?
        Intervene. O descend as a dove or
A furious papa or a mild engineer, but descend.'

And the life, if it answers at all, replies from the heart
And the eyes and the lungs, from the shops and squares of
                                        the city:
        'O no, I am not the mover;
Not to-day; not to you. To you, I'm the

'Yes-man, the bar-companion, the easily-duped;
I am whatever you do. I am your vow to be
        Good, your humorous story.
I am your business voice. I am your marriage.

'What's your proposal? To build the just city? I will.
I agree. Or is it the suicide pact, the romantic
        Death? Very well, I accept, for
I am your choice, your decision. Yes, I am Spain.'

Many have heard it on remote peninsulas,
On sleepy plains, in the aberrant fisherman's islands
        Or the corrupt heart of the city,
Have heard and migrated like gulls or the seeds of a
                                        flower.

They clung like birds to the long expresses that lurch
Through the unjust lands, through the night, through the
alpine tunnel;
They floated over the oceans;
They walked the passes. All presented their lives.

On that arid square, that fragment nipped off from hot
Africa, soldered so crudely to inventive Europe;
On that tableland scored by rivers,
Our thoughts have bodies; the menacing shapes of our
fever

Are precise and alive. For the fears which made us
respond
To the medicine ad. and the brochure of winter cruises
Have become invading battalions;
And our faces, the institute-face, the chain-store, the ruin

Are projecting their greed as the firing squad and the
bomb.
Madrid is the heart. Our moments of tenderness blossom
As the ambulance and the sandbag;
Our hours of friendship into a people's army.

To-morrow, perhaps the future. The research on fatigue
And the movements of packers; the gradual exploring of
all the
Octaves of radiation;
To-morrow the enlarging of consciousness by diet and
breathing.

To-morrow the rediscovery of romantic love,
The photographing of ravens; all the fun under
      Liberty's masterful shadow;
To-morrow the hour of the pageant-master and the
                        musician,

The beautiful roar of the chorus under the dome;
To-morrow the exchanging of tips on the breeding of
                        terriers,
      The eager election of chairmen
By the sudden forest of hands. But to-day the struggle.

To-morrow for the young the poets exploding like bombs,
The walks by the lake, the weeks of perfect communion;
      To-morrow the bicycle races
Through the suburbs on summer evenings. But to-day
                        the struggle.

To-day the deliberate increase in the chances of death,
The conscious acceptance of guilt in the necessary murder;
      To-day the expending of powers
On the flat ephemeral pamphlet and the boring meeting.

To-day the makeshift consolations: the shared cigarette,
The cards in the candlelit barn, and the scraping concert,
      The masculine jokes; to-day the
Fumbled and unsatisfactory embrace before hurting.

The stars are dead. The animals will not look.
We are left alone with our day, and the time is short, and
      History to the defeated
May say Alas but cannot help nor pardon.

IN MEMORY OF SIGMUND FREUD

(d. Sept. 1939)

When there are so many we shall have to mourn,
When grief has been made so public, and exposed
    To the critique of a whole epoch
    The frailty of our conscience and anguish,

Of whom shall we speak? For every day they die
Among us, those who were doing us some good,
    And knew it was never enough but
    Hoped to improve a little by living.

Such was this doctor: still at eighty he wished
To think of our life, from whose unruliness
    So many plausible young futures
    With threats of flattery ask obedience.

But his wish was denied him; he closed his eyes
Upon that last picture common to us all,
    Of problems like relatives standing
    Puzzled and jealous about our dying.

For about him at the very end were still
Those he had studied, the nervous and the nights,
    And shades that still waited to enter
    The bright circle of his recognition

Turned elsewhere with their disappointment as he
Was taken away from his old interest

To go back to the earth in London,
An important Jew who died in exile.

Only Hate was happy, hoping to augment
His practice now, and his shabby clientele
        Who think they can be cured by killing
        And covering the gardens with ashes.

They are still alive but in a world he changed
Simply by looking back with no false regrets;
        All that he did was to remember
        Like the old and be honest like children.

He wasn't clever at all: he merely told
The unhappy Present to recite the Past
        Like a poetry lesson till sooner
        Or later it faltered at the line where

Long ago the accusations had begun,
And suddenly knew by whom it had been judged,
        How rich life had been and how silly,
        And was life-forgiven and more humble.

Able to approach the Future as a friend
Without a wardrobe of excuses, without
        A set mask of rectitude or an
        Embarrassing over-familiar gesture.

No wonder the ancient cultures of conceit
In his technique of unsettlement foresaw
        The fall of princes, the collapse of
        Their lucrative patterns of frustration.

If he succeeded, why, the Generalised Life
Would become impossible, the monolith
        Of State be broken and prevented
        The co-operation of avengers.

Of course they called on God: but he went his way,
Down among the Lost People like Dante, down
        To the stinking fosse where the injured
        Lead the ugly life of the rejected.

And showed us what evil is: not as we thought
Deeds that must be punished, but our lack of faith,
        Our dishonest mood of denial,
        The concupiscence of the oppressor.

And if something of the autocratic pose,
The paternal strictness he distrusted, still
        Clung to his utterance and features,
        It was a protective imitation.

For one who lived among enemies so long:
If often he was wrong and at times absurd,
        To us he is no more a person
        Now but a whole climate of opinion.

Under whom we conduct our differing lives:
Like weather he can only hinder or help,
        The proud can still be proud but find it
        A little harder, and the tyrant tries

To make him do but doesn't care for him much.
He quietly surrounds all our habits of growth;

He extends, till the tired in even
The remotest most miserable duchy

Have felt the change in their bones and are cheered,
And the child unlucky in his little State,
        Some hearth where freedom is excluded,
        A hive whose honey is fear and worry,

Feels calmer now and somehow assured of escape;
While as they lie in the grass of our neglect,
        So many long-forgotten objects
        Revealed by his undiscouraged shining

Are returned to us and made precious again;
Games we had thought we must drop as we grew up,
        Little noises we dared not laugh at,
        Faces we made when no one was looking.

But he wishes us more than this: to be free
Is often to be lonely; he would unite
        The unequal moieties fractured
        By our own well-meaning sense of justice.

Would restore to the larger the wit and will
The smaller possesses but can only use
        For arid disputes, would give back to
        The son the mother's richness of feeling.

But he would have us remember most of all
To be enthusiastic over the night

Not only for the sense of wonder
It alone has to offer, but also

Because it needs our love: for with sad eyes
Its delectable creatures look up and beg
    Us dumbly to ask them to follow;
    They are exiles who long for the future

That lies in our power. They too would rejoice
If allowed to serve enlightenment like him,
    Even to bear our cry of 'Judas',
    As he did and all must bear who serve it.

One rational voice is dumb: over a grave
The household of Impulse mourns one dearly loved.
    Sad is Eros, builder of cities,
    And weeping of anarchic Aphrodite.

CECIL DAY LEWIS

"SUPPOSE THAT WE"

Suppose that we, to-morrow or the next day,
Came to an end—in storm the shafting broken,
Or a mistaken signal, the flange lifting—
Would that be premature, a text for sorrow?

Say what endurance gives or death denies us.
Love's proved in its creation, not eternity:
Like leaf or linnet the true heart's affection
Is born, dies later, asks no reassurance.

Over dark wood rises one dawn felicitous,
Bright through awakened shadows fall her crystal
Cadenzas, and once for all the wood is quickened.
So our joys visit us, and it suffices.

Nor fear we now to live who in the valley
Of the shadow of life have found a causeway;
For love restores the nerve and love is under
Our feet resilient. Shall we be weary?

Some say we walk out of Time altogether
This way into a region where the primrose

Shows an immortal dew, sun at meridian
Stands up for ever and in scent the lime tree.

This is a land which later we may tell of.
Here-now we know, what death cannot diminish
Needs no replenishing; yet certain are, though
Dying were well enough, to live is better.

Passion has grown full man by his first birthday.
Running across the bean-fields in a south wind,
Fording the river mouth to feel the tide-race—
Child's play that was, though proof of our possessions.

Now our research is done, measured the shadow,
The plains mapped out, the hills a natural bound'ry.
Such and such is our country. There remains to
Plough up the meadowland, reclaim the marshes.

"REST FROM LOVING"

Rest from loving and be living.
Fallen is fallen past retrieving
The unique flyer dawn's dove
Arrowing down feathered with fire.

Cease denying, begin knowing.
Comes peace this way here comes renewing
With dower of bird and bud knocks
Loud on winter wall on death's door.

Here's no meaning but of morning.
Naught soon of night but stars remaining,
Sink lower, fade, as dark womb
Recedes creation will step clear.

"AS ONE WHO WANDERS"

As one who wanders into old workings
Dazed by the noonday, desiring coolness,
Has found retreat barred by fall of rockface;
Gropes through galleries where granite bruises
Taut palm and panic patters close at heel;
Must move forward as tide to the moon's nod,
As mouth to breast in blindness is beckoned.
Nightmare nags at his elbow and narrows
Horizon to pinpoint, hope to hand's breadth.
Slow drip the seconds, time is stalactite,
For nothing intrudes here to tell the time,
Sun marches not, nor moon with muffled step.
He wants an opening,—only to break out,
To see the dark glass cut by day's diamond,
To relax again in the lap of light.

But we seek a new world through old workings,
Whose hope lies like seed in the loins of earth,
Whose dawn draws gold from the roots of darkness.
Not shy of light nor shrinking from shadow
Like Jesuits in jungle we journey
Deliberately bearing to brutish tribes
Christ's assurance, arts of agriculture.

As a train that travels underground track
Feels current flashed from far-off dynamos,
Our wheels whirling with impetus elsewhere
Generated we run, are ruled by rails.
Train shall spring from tunnel to terminus,
Out on to plain shall the pioneer plunge,
Earth reveal what veins fed, what hill covered.
Lovely the leap, explosion into light.

"MORE THAN ALL ELSE"

More than all else might you,
My son, my daughter,
Be metal to bore through
The impermeable clay
And rock that overlay
The living water.

Through that artesian well
My self may out,
Finding its own level.
This way the waste land turns
To arable, and towns
Are rid of drought.

"DO NOT EXPECT AGAIN"

Do not expect again a phœnix hour,
The triple-towered sky, the dove complaining,
Sudden the rain of gold and heart's first ease
Tranced under trees by the eldritch light of sundown.

By a blazed trail our joy will be returning:
One burning hour throws light a thousand ways,
And hot blood stays into familiar gestures.
The best years wait, the body's plenitude.

Consider then, my lover, this is the end
Of the lark's ascending, the hawk's unearthly hover:
Spring season is over soon and first heatwave;
Grave-browed with cloud ponders the huge horizon.

Draw up the dew. Swell with pacific violence.
Take shape in silence. Grow as the clouds grew.
Beautiful brood the cornlands, and you are heavy;
Leafy the boughs—they also hide big fruit.

"NEARING AGAIN THE LEGENDARY ISLE"

Nearing again the legendary isle
Where sirens sang and mariners were skinned,
We wonder now what was there to beguile
That such stout fellows left their bones behind.

Those chorus-girls are surely past their prime,
Voices grow shrill and paint is wearing thin,
Lips that sealed up the sense from gnawing time
Now beg the favour with a graveyard grin.

We have no flesh to spare and they can't bite,
Hunger and sweat have stripped us to the bone;
A skeleton crew we toil upon the tide
And mock the theme-song meant to lure us on:

No need to stop the ears, avert the eyes
From purple rhetoric of evening skies.

"LET US NOW PRAISE"

Second Defendant speaks
 Let us now praise famous men,
 Not your earth-shakers, not the dynamiters,
 But who in the Home Counties or the Khyber,
 Trimming their nails to meet an ill wind,
 Facing the Adversary with a clean collar,
 Justified the system.
 Admire the venerable pile that bred them,
 Bones are its foundations,
 The pinnacles are stone abstractions,
 Whose halls are whispering-galleries designed
 To echo voices of the past, dead tongues.
 White hopes of England here
 Are taught to rule by learning to obey,
 Bend over before vested interests,
 Kiss the rod, salute the quarter-deck;
 Here is no savage discipline
 Of peregrine swooping, of fire destroying,
 But a civil code; no capital offender
 But the cool cad, the man who goes too far.
 Ours the curriculum
 Neither of building birds nor wasteful waters,
 Bound in book not violent in vein:
 Here we inoculate with dead ideas
 Against blood-epidemics, against

The infection of faith and the excess of life.
Our methods are up to date; we teach
Through head and not by heart,
Language with gramophones and sex with charts,
Prophecy by deduction, prayer by numbers.
For honours see prospectus: those who leave us
Will get a post and pity the poor;
Their eyes glaze at strangeness;
They are never embarrassed, have a word for
                                    everything,
Living on credit, dying when the heart stops;
Will wear black armlets and stand a moment in
                                    silence
For the passing of an era, at their own funeral.

"TO SIT AT HEAD OF ONE'S OWN TABLE"

Fourth Defendant speaks
To sit at head of one's own table,
To overlook a warm familiar landscape,
Have large cupboards for small responsibilities—
Surely that does outweigh
The rent veil and the agonies to follow?
Me the Almighty fixed, from Eve fallen,
Heart-deep in earth, a pointer to star fields,
Suffering sapflow, fruitage, early barrenness;
Changeable reputed, but to change constant,
Fickle of fashion no more than the months are;
Daily depend on surroundings for sustenance,
On what my roots reach, what my leaves inhale here.

Grant me a rich ground, wrapped in airs temperate,
Not where nor'-easters threaten the flint scarps;
Consequence then shall I have, men's admiration
Now, and my bones shall be fuel for the future.
Yet have I always failed.
For he, who should have been my prime possession,
Was not to be possessed.
I leant o'er him, a firmament of shadow,
But he looked up through me and saw the stars.
I would have bound him in the earth-ways,
Fluid, immediate, the child of nature.
But he made bricks of earth, iron from fire,
Turned waves to power, winds to communication;
Setting up Art against Chaos, subjecting
My flux to the synthetic frost of reason.
I am left with a prone man,
Virtue gone out of him; who in the morning
Will rise to join Crusades or assist the Harlequins.
Though I persuade him that his stars are mine eyes'
Refraction, that wisdom's best expressed in
The passive mood,—here's no change for the better:
I was the body slave, am now the spirit's.
Come let me contemplate my own
Mysteries, a dark glass may save my face.

"YOU THAT LOVE ENGLAND"

You that love England, who have an ear for her music,
The slow movement of clouds in benediction,
Clear arias of light thrilling over her uplands,

Over the chords of summer sustained peacefully;
Ceaseless the leaves' counterpoint in a west wind lively,
Blossom and river rippling loveliest allegro,
And the storms of wood strings brass at year's finale:
Listen. Can you not hear the entrance of a new theme?

You who go out alone, on tandem or on pillion,
Down arterial roads riding in April,
Or sad beside lakes where hill-slopes are reflected
Making fires of leaves, your high hopes fallen:
Cyclists and hikers in company, day excursionists,
Refugees from cursed towns and devastated areas;
Know you seek a new world, a saviour to establish
Long-lost kinship and restore the blood's fulfilment.

You who like peace, good sticks, happy in a small way
Watching birds or playing cricket with schoolboys,
Who pay for drinks all round, whom disaster chose not;
Yet passing derelict mills and barns roof-rent
Where despair has burnt itself out—hearts at a standstill,
Who suffer loss, aware of lowered vitality;
We can tell you a secret, offer a tonic; only
Submit to the visiting angel, the strange new healer.

You above all who have come to the far end, victims
Of a run-down machine, who can bear it no longer;
Whether in easy chairs chafing at impotence
Or against hunger, bullies and spies preserving
The nerve for action, the spark of indignation—

Need fight in the dark no more, you know your enemies.
You shall be leaders when zero hour is signalled,
Wielders of power and welders of a new world.

A TIME TO DANCE

For those who had the power
    of the forest fires that burn
Leaving their source in ashes
    to flush the sky with fire:
Those whom a famous urn
    could not contain, whose passion
Brimmed over the deep grave
    and dazzled epitaphs:
For all that have won us wings
    to clear the tops of grief,
My friend who within me laughs
    bids you dance and sing.

Some set out to explore
    earth's limit, and little they recked if
Never their feet came near it
    outgrowing the need for glory:
Some aimed at a small objective
    but the fierce updraught of their spirit
Forced them to the stars.
    Are honoured in public who built
The dam that tamed a river;
    or holding the salient for hours
Against odds, cut off and killed,
    are remembered by one survivor.

All these. But most for those
　　whom accident made great,
As a radiant chance encounter
　　of cloud and sunlight grows
Immortal on the heart:
　　whose gift was the sudden bounty
Of a passing moment, enriches
　　the fulfilled eye for ever.
Their spirits float serene
　　above time's roughest reaches,
But their seed is in us and over
　　our lives they are evergreen.

OVERTURES TO DEATH

It is not you I fear, but the humiliations
You mercifully use to deaden grief—
The downward graph of natural joys,
Imagination's slump, the blunted ear.

I hate this cold and politic self-defence
Of hardening arteries and nerves
Grown dull with time-serving. I see that the heart lives
By self-betrayal, by circumspection is killed.

That boy, whose glance makes heaven open and edges
Each dawning pain with gold, must learn to disbelieve:
The wildfire lust of the eyes will gutter down
To age's dim recalcitrance.

Have we not seen how quick this young girl's thoughts,
Wayward and burning as a charm of goldfinches
Alarmed from thistle-tops, turn into
Spite or a cupboard love or clipped routine?

Nearing the watershed and the difficult passes,
Man wraps up closer against the chill
In his familiar habits; and at the top
Pauses, seeing your kingdom like a net beneath him spread.

Some climbed to this momentous peak of the world
And facing the horizon—that notorious pure woman
Who lures to cheat the last embrace,
Hurled themselves down upon an easier doom.

One the rare air made dizzy renounced
Earth, and the avalanche took him at his word:
One wooed perfection—he's bedded deep in the glacier,
                              perfect
And null, the prince and image of despair.

The best, neither hoarding nor squandering
The radiant flesh and the receptive
Spirit, stepped on together in the rhythm of comrades
                              who
Have found a route on earth's true reckoning based.

They have not known the false humility,
The shamming-dead of the senses beneath your hunter's
                              hand;
But life's green standards they've advanced
To the limit of your salt unyielding zone.

WHEN THEY HAVE LOST

When they have lost the little that they looked for,
The poor allotment of ease, custom, fame:
When the consuming star their fathers worked for
Has guttered into death, a fatuous flame:
When love's a cripple, faith a bed-time story,
Hope eats her heart out and peace walks on knives,
And suffering men cry an end to this sorry
World of whose children want alone still thrives:
Then shall the mounting stages of oppression
Like mazed and makeshift scaffolding torn down
Reveal his unexampled, best creation—
The shape of man's necessity full-grown.
Built from their bone, I see a power-house stand
To warm men's hearts again and light the land.

IN THE HEART OF CONTEMPLATION

In the heart of contemplation—
Admiring, say, the frost-flowers of the white lilac,
Or lark's song busily sifting like sand-crystals
Through the pleased hourglass an afternoon of summer,
Or your beauty, dearer to me than these—
Discreetly a whisper in the ear,
The glance of one passing my window recall me
From lark, lilac, you, grown suddenly strangers.

In the plump and pastoral valley
Of a leisure time, among the trees like seabirds

Asleep on a glass calm, one shadow moves—
The sly reminder of the forgotten appointment.
All the shining pleasures, born to be innocent,
Grow dark with a truant's guilt:
The day's high heart falls flat, the oaks tremble,
And the shadow sliding over your face divides us.

In the act of decision only,
In the hearts cleared for action like lovers naked
For love, this shadow vanishes: there alone
There is nothing between our lives for it to thrive on.
You and I with lilac, lark and oak-leafed
Valley are bound together
As in the astounded clarity before death.
Nothing is innocent now but to act for life's sake.

BEHOLD THE SWAN

Behold the swan
Riding at her image, anchored there
Complacent, a water-lily upon
The ornamental water:
Queen of the mute October air,
She broods in that unbroken
Reverie of reed and water.

Now from the stricken
Pool she hoists and flurries,
And passes overhead
In hoarse, expressive flight:

Her wings bear hard
On the vibrant air: unhurried
The threat and pulse of wings, the throat
Levelled towards the horizon, see—
They are prophecy.

O DREAMS, O DESTINATIONS

For infants time is like a humming shell
Heard between sleep and sleep, wherein the shores
Foam-fringed, wind-fluted of the strange earth dwell
And the sea's cavernous hunger faintly roars.
It is the humming pole of summer lanes
Whose sound quivers like heat-haze endlessly
Over the corn, over the poppied plains—
An emanation from the earth or sky.
Faintly they hear, through the womb's lingering haze,
A rumour of that sea to which they are born:
They hear the ringing pole of summer days,
But need not know what hungers for the corn.
They are the lisping rushes in a stream—
Grace-notes of a profound, legato dream.

Children look down upon the morning-grey
Tissue of mist that veils a valley's lap:
Their fingers itch to tear it and unwrap
The flags, the roundabouts,the gala day.
They watch the spring rise inexhaustibly—
A breathing thread out of the eddied sand,
Sufficient to their day: but half their mind
Is on the sailed and glittering estuary.

Fondly we wish their mist might never break,
Knowing it hides so much that best were hidden:
We'd chain them by the spring, lest it should broaden
For them into a quicksand and a wreck.
But they slip through our fingers like the source.
Like mist, like time that has flagged out their course.

That was the fatal move, the ruination
Of innocence so innocently begun,
When in the lawless orchard of creation
The child left this fruit for that rosier one.
Reaching towards the far thing, we begin it;
Looking beyond, or backward, more and more
We grow unfaithful to the unique minute
Till, from neglect, its features stale and blur.
Fish, bird or beast was never thus unfaithful—
Man only casts the image of his joys
Beyond his senses' reach; and by this fateful
Act, he confirms the ambiguous power of choice.
Innocence made that first choice. It is she
Who weeps, a child chained to the outraged tree.

Our youthtime passes down a colonnade
Shafted with alternating light and shade.
All's dark or dazzle there. Half in a dream
Rapturously we move, yet half afraid
Never to wake. That diamond-point, extreme
Brilliance engraved on us a classic theme:
The shaft of darkness had its lustre too,
Rising where earth's concentric mysteries gleam.
Oh youth-charmed hours, that made an avenue

Of fountains playing us on to love's full view,
A cypress walk to some romantic grave—
Waking, how false in outline and in hue
We find the dreams that flickered on our cave:
Only your fire, which cast them, still seems true.

All that time there was thunder in the air:
Our nerves branched and flickered with summer lightning.
The taut crab-apple, the pampas quivering, the glare
On the roses seemed irrelevant, or a heightening
At most of the sealed-up hour wherein we awaited
What?—some explosive oracle to abash
The platitudes on the lawn? heaven's delegated
Angel—the golden rod, our burning bush?
No storm broke. Yet in retrospect the rose
Mounting vermilion, fading, glowing again
Like a fire's heart, that breathless inspiration
Of pampas grass, crab-tree's attentive pose
Never were so divinely charged as then—
The veiled Word's flesh, a near annunciation.

Symbols of gross experience!—our grief
Flowed, like a sacred river, underground:
Desire bred fierce abstractions on the mind,
Then like an eagle soared beyond belief.
Often we tried our breast against the thorn,
Our paces on the turf: whither we flew,
Why we should agonize, we hardly knew—
Nor what ached in us, asking to be born.
Ennui of youth!—thin air above the clouds,
Vain divination of the sunless stream

Mirror that impotence, till we redeem
Our birthright, and the shadowplay concludes.
Ah, not in dreams, but when our souls engage
With the common mesh and moil, we come of age.

Older, we build a road where once our active
Heat threw up mountains and the deep dales veined:
We're glad to gain the limited objective,
Knowing the war we fight in has no end.
The road must needs follow each contour moulded
By that fire in its losing fight with earth:
We march over our past, we may behold it
Dreaming a slave's dream on our bivouac hearth.
Lost the archaic dawn wherein we started,
The appetite for wholeness: now we prize
Half-loaves, half-truths—enough for the half-hearted,
The gleam snatched from corruption satisfies.
Dead youth, forgive us if, all but defeated,
We raise a trophy where your honour lies.

But look, the old illusion still returns,
Walking a field-path where the succory burns
Like summer's eye, blue lustre-drops of noon,
And the heart follows it and freshly yearns:
Yearns to the sighing distances beyond
Each height of happiness, the vista drowned
In gold-dust haze, and dreams itself immune
From change and night to which all else is bound.
Love, we have caught perfection for a day
As succory holds a gem of halcyon ray:
Summer burns out, its flower will tarnish soon—

Deathless illusion, that could so relay
The truth of flesh and spirit, sun and clay
Singing for once together all in tune!

To travel like a bird, lightly to view
Deserts where stone gods founder in the sand,
Ocean embraced in a white sleep with land;
To escape time, always to start anew.
To settle like a bird, make one devoted
Gesture of permanence upon the spray
Of shaken stars and autumns; in a bay
Beyond the crestfallen surges to have floated.
Each is our wish. Alas, the bird flies blind,
Hooded by a dark sense of destination:
Her weight on the glass calm leaves no impression,
Her home is soon a basketful of wind.
Travellers, we're fabric of the road we go;
We settle, but like feathers on time's flow.

THE IMAGE

From far, she seemed to lie like a stone on the sick horizon:
Too soon that face, intolerably near,
Writhed like a furious ant-hill. Whoever, they say, set
                                       eyes on
Her face became a monument to fear.

But Perseus, lifting his shield, beheld as in a view-finder
A miniature monster, darkly illustrious.
Absorbed, pitying perhaps, he struck. And the sky behind
                                         her
Woke with a healthier colour, purified thus.

Now, in a day of monsters, a desert of abject stone
Whose outward terrors paralyse the will,
Look to that gleaming circle until it has revealed you

The glare of death transmuted to your own
Measure, scaled-down to a possible figure the sum of ill.
Let the shield take that image, the image shield you.

WHERE ARE THE WAR POETS?

They who in folly or mere greed
Enslaved religion, markets, laws,
Borrow our language now and bid
Us to speak up in freedom's cause.

It is the logic of our times,
No subject for immortal verse—
That we who lived by honest dreams
Defend the bad against the worse.

THE REBUKE

Down in the lost and April days
What lies we told, what lies we told!
Nakedness seemed the one disgrace,
And there'd be time enough to praise
The truth when we were old.

The irresponsible poets sung
What came into their head:
Time to pick and choose among
The bold profusions of our tongue
When we were dead, when we were dead.

Oh wild the words we uttered then
In woman's ear, in woman's ear,
Believing all we promised when
Each kiss created earth again
And every far was near.

Little we guessed, who spoke the word
Of hope and freedom high
Spontaneously as wind or bird
To crowds like cornfields still or stirred,
It was a lie, a heart-felt lie.

Now the years advance into
A calmer stream, a colder stream,
We doubt the flame that once we knew,
Heroic words sound all untrue
As love-lies in a dream.

Yet fools are the old who won't be taught
Modesty by their youth:
That pandemonium of the heart,
That sensual arrogance did impart
A kind of truth, a kindling truth.

Where are the sparks at random sown,
The spendthrift fire, the holy fire?
Who cares a damn for truth that's grown
Exhausted haggling for its own
And speaks without desire?

STEPHEN SPENDER

"NEVER BEING, BUT ALWAYS"

Never being, but always at the edge of Being
My head, like Death-mask is brought into the sun.
The shadow pointing finger across cheek,
I move lips for tasting, I move hands for touching,
But never am nearer than touching
Though the spirit lean outward for seeing.
Observing rose, gold, eyes, an admired landscape,
My senses record the act of wishing
Wishing to be
Rose, gold, landscape or another.
I claim fulfilment in the fact of loving.

THE PRISONERS

Far far the least of all, in want,
Are these,
The prisoners
Turned massive with their vaults and dark with dark.

They raise no hands, which rest upon their knees,
But lean their solid eyes against the night,
Dimly they feel
Only the furniture they use in cells.

Their Time is almost Death. The silted flow
Of years on years
Is marked by dawns
As faint as cracks on mud-flats of despair.

My pity moves amongst them like a breeze
On walls of stone
Fretting for summer leaves, or like a tune
On ears of stone.

Then, when I raise my hands to strike,
It is too late,
There are no chains that fall
Nor visionary liquid door
Melted with anger.

When have their lives been free from walls and dark
And airs that choke?
And where less prisoner to let my anger
Like a sun strike?

If I could follow them from room to womb
To plant some hope
Through the black silk of the big-bellied gown
There would I win.

No, no, no,
It is too late for anger,
Nothing prevails
But pity for the grief they cannot feel.

"I THINK CONTINUALLY OF THOSE"

I think continually of those who were truly great.
Who, from the womb, remembered the soul's history
Through corridors of light where the hours are suns
Endless and singing. Whose lovely ambition
Was that their lips, still touched with fire,
Should tell of the Spirit clothed from head to foot in song.
And who hoarded from the Spring branches
The desires falling across their bodies like blossoms.

What is precious is never to forget
The essential delight of the blood drawn from ageless
                                        springs
Breaking through rocks in worlds before our earth.
Never to deny its pleasure in the morning simple light
Nor its grave evening demand for love.
Never to allow gradually the traffic to smother
With noise and fog the flowering of the spirit.

Near the snow, near the sun, in the highest fields
See how these names are fêted by the waving grass
And by the streamers of white cloud
And whispers of wind in the listening sky.
The names of those who in their lives fought for life
Who wore at their hearts the fire's centre.
Born of the sun they travelled a short while towards
                                        the sun,
And left the vivid air signed with their honour.

"AFTER THEY HAVE TIRED"

After they have tired of the brilliance of cities
And of striving for office where at last they may
                                        languish
Hung round with easy chains until
Death and Jerusalem glorify also the crossing-sweeper:
Then those streets the rich built and their easy love
Fade like old cloths, and it is death stalks through life
Grinning white through all faces
Clean and equal like the shine from snow.

In this time when grief pours freezing over us,
When the hard light of pain gleams at every street corner,
When those who were pillars of that day's gold roof
Shrink in their clothes; surely from hunger
We may strike fire, like fire from flint?
And our strength is now the strength of our bones
Clean and equal like the shine from snow
And the strength of famine and of our enforced idleness,
And it is the strength of our love for each other.

Readers of this strange language,
We have come at last to a country
Where light equal, like the shine from snow, strikes all
                                        faces,
Here you may wonder
How it was that works, money, interest, building, could
                                        ever hide
The palpable and obvious love of man for man.

Oh comrades, let not those who follow after
—The beautiful generation that shall spring from our
sides—
Let not them wonder how after the failure of banks
The failure of cathedrals and the declared insanity of
our rulers,
We lacked the Spring-like resources of the tiger
Or of plants who strike out new roots to gushing
waters.
But through torn-down portions of old fabric let their
eyes
Watch the admiring dawn explode like a shell
Around us, dazing us with its light like snow.

THE FUNERAL

Death is another milestone on their way.
With laughter on their lips and with winds blowing
round them
They record simply
How this one excelled all others in making driving belts.

This is festivity, it is the time of statistics
When they record what one unit contributed:
They are glad as they lay him back in the earth
And thank him for what he gave them.

They walk home remembering the straining red flags,
And with pennons of song still fluttering through
their blood

They speak of the world state
With its towns like brain-centres and its pulsing arteries.

They think how one life hums, revolves and toils,
One cog in a golden and singing hive:
Like spark from fire, its task happily achieved,
It falls away quietly.

No more are they haunted by the individual grief
Nor the crocodile tears of European genius,
The decline of a culture
Mourned by scholars who dream of the ghosts of Greek
                                        boys.

THE EXPRESS

After the first powerful plain manifesto
The black statement of pistons, without more fuss
But gliding like a queen she leaves the station
Without bowing and with restrained unconcern
She passes the houses which humbly crowd outside,
The gasworks and at last the heavy page
Of death, printed by gravestones in the cemetery.
Beyond the town there lies the open country
Where, gathering speed, she acquires mystery,
The luminous self-possession of ships on ocean.
It is now she begins to sing—at first quite low
Then loud, and at last with a jazzy madness—
The song of her whistle screaming at curves,
Of deafening tunnels, brakes, innumerable bolts.
And always light, aerial, underneath

Goes the elate metre of her wheels.
Steaming through metal landscape on her lines
She plunges new eras of wild happiness
Where speed throws up strange shapes, broad curves
And parallels clean like the steel of guns.
At last, further than Edinburgh or Rome,
Beyond the crest of the world, she reaches night
Where only a low streamline brightness
Of phosphorus on the tossing hills is white.
Ah, like a comet through flame she moves entranced
Wrapt in her music no bird song, no, nor bough
Breaking with honey buds, shall ever equal.

THE PYLONS

The secret of these hills was stone, and cottages
Of that stone made,
And crumbling roads
That turned on sudden hidden villages.

Now over these small hills they have built the concrete
That trails black wire:
Pylons, those pillars
Bare like nude, giant girls that have no secret.

The valley with its gilt and evening look
And the green chestnut
Of customary root
Are mocked dry like the parched bed of a brook.

But far above and far as sight endures
Like whips of anger
With lightning's danger
There runs the quick perspective of the future.

This dwarfs our emerald country by its trek
So tall with prophecy:
Dreaming of cities
Where often clouds shall lean their swan-white neck.

"IN RAILWAY HALLS"

In railway halls, on pavements near the traffic,
They beg, their eyes made big by empty staring
And only measuring Time, like the blank clock.

No, I shall weave no tracery of pen-ornament
To make them birds upon my singing-tree:
Time merely drives these lives which do not live
As tides push rotten stuff along the shore.

—There is no consolation, no, none
In the curving beauty of that line
Traced on our graphs through history, where the
                                         oppressor
Starves and deprives the poor.

Paint here no draped despairs, no saddening clouds
Where the soul rests, proclaims eternity.
But let the wrong cry out as raw as wounds
This Time forgets and never heals, far less transcends.

"NOT PALACES, AN ERA'S CROWN"

Not palaces, an era's crown
Where the mind dwells, intrigues, rests;
The architectural gold-leaved flower
From people ordered like a single mind,
I build. This only what I tell:
It is too late for rare accumulation
For family pride, for beauty's filtered dusts;
I say, stamping the words with emphasis,
Drink from here energy and only energy,
As from the electric charge of a battery,
To will this Time's change.
Eye, gazelle, delicate wanderer,
Drinker of horizon's fluid line;
Ear that suspends on a chord
The spirit drinking timelessness;
Touch, love, all senses;
Leave your gardens, your singing feasts,
Your dreams of suns circling before our sun,
Of heaven after our world.
Instead, watch images of flashing brass.
That strike the outward sense, the polished will
Flag of our purpose which the wind engraves.
No spirit seek here rest. But this: No man
Shall hunger: Man shall spend equally.
Our goal which we compel: Man shall be man.

—That programme of the antique Satan
Bristling with guns on the indented page

With battleship towering from hilly waves:
For what? Drive of a ruining purpose
Destroying all but its age-long exploiters.
Our programme like this, yet opposite,
Death to the killers, bringing light to life.

POLAR EXPLORATION

Our single purpose was to walk through snow
With faces swung to their prodigious North
Like compass iron. As clerks in whited banks
With bird-claw pens column virgin paper,
To snow we added foot-prints.
Extensive whiteness drowned
All sense of space. We tramped through
Static, glaring days, Time's suspended blank.
That was in Spring and Autumn. Summer struck
Water over rocks, and half the world
Became a ship with a deep keel, the booming floes
And icebergs with their little birds:
Twittering Snow Bunting, Greenland Wheatear,
Red-throated Divers; imagine butterflies
Sulphurous cloudy yellow; glory of bees
That suck from saxifrage; crowberry,
Bilberry, cranberry, *Pyrola Uniflora*.
There followed Winter in a frozen hut
Warm enough at the kernel, but dare to sleep
With head against the wall—ice gummed my hair!
Hate Culver's loud breathing, despise Freeman's
Fidget for washing: love only the dogs

That whine for scraps, and scratch. Notice
How they run better (on short journeys) with a bitch.
In that, different from us.
Return, return, you warn. We do. There is
A network of railways, money, words, words, words.
Meals, papers, exchanges, debates,
Cinema, wireless: the worst, is Marriage.
We cannot sleep. At night we watch
A speaking clearness through cloudy paranoia.
These questions are white rifts:—Was
Ice our anger transformed? The raw, the motionless
Skies, were these the Spirit's hunger?
The continual and hypnotized march through snow,
The dropping nights of precious extinction, were these
Only the wide inventions of the will,
The frozen will's evasion? If this exists
In us as madness here, as coldness
In these summer, civilized sheets: Is the North,
Over there, a tangible, real madness,
A glittering simpleton, one without towns,
Only with bears and fish, a staring eye,
A new and singular sex?

AN ELEMENTARY SCHOOL CLASS
ROOM IN A SLUM

Far, far from gusty waves, these children's faces.
Like rootless weeds the torn hair round their paleness.
The tall girl with her weighed-down head. The paper-
seeming boy with rat's eyes. The stunted unlucky heir

Of twisted bones, reciting a father's gnarled disease,
His lesson from his desk. At back of the dim class,
One unnoted, sweet and young: his eyes live in a dream
Of squirrels' game, in tree room, other than this.

On sour cream walls, donations. Shakespeare's head
Cloudless at dawn, civilized dome riding all cities.
Belled, flowery, Tyrolese valley. Open-handed map
Awarding the world its world.And yet, for these
Children, these windows, not this world, are world,
Where all their future's painted with a fog,
A narrow street sealed in with a lead sky,
Far far from rivers, capes, and stars of words.

Surely Shakespeare is wicked, the map a bad example
With ships and sun and love tempting them to steal—
For lives that slyly turn in their cramped holes
From fog to endless night? On their slag heap, these
                                    children
Wear skins peeped through by bones and spectacles of
                                    steel
With mended glass, like bottle bits on stones.
All of their time and space are foggy slum
So blot their maps with slums as big as doom.

Unless, governor, teacher, inspector, visitor,
This map becomes their window and these windows
That open on their lives like crouching tombs
Break, O break open, till they break the town
And show the children to the fields and all their world

Azure on their sands, to let their tongues
Run naked into books, the white and green leaves open
The history theirs whose language is the sun.

THE UNCREATING CHAOS

I

To the hanging despair of eyes in the street, offer
Your making hands and your guts on skewers of pity.
When the pyramid sky is piled with clouds of sand
                                which the yellow
Sun blasts above, respond to that day's doom
With a headache. Let your ghost follow
The young men to the Pole, up Everest, to war: by love,
                                be shot,

For the uncreating chaos descends
And claims you in marriage: though a man, you were
                                ever a bride:
Ever beneath the supple surface of summer muscle,
The fountain evening talk cupping the summer stars,
The student who chucks back the lock from his hair in
                                front of a silver glass,
You were only anxious that all these passions should last.

The engine in you, anxiety,
Was a grave lecher, a glove-trotter, one
Whose moods were straws, the winds that puffed them,
                                aeroplanes.

'Whatever happens, I shall never be alone,
I shall always have an affair, a railway fare, or a
                            revolution.'

Without your buttressing gesture that yet so leans;
Is glad as a mat
When stamped on; blood that gives suck to a vampire
                            bat;
And your heart fretted by winds like rocks at Land's
                            End:
You'd stand alone in a silence that never uttered
And stare in yourself as though on a desolate room.

IV

Shall I never reach
The field guarded by stones
Precious in the stone mountains,
Where the scytheless wind
Flushes the warm grasses:
Where clouds without rain
Add to the sun
Their lucid sailing shine?
The simple mechanism is here,
Clear day, thoughts of the work-room, the desk,
The hand, symbols of power.
Here the veins may pour
Into the deed, as the field
Into the standing corn.
Meanwhile, where nothing's pious

And life no longer willed,
Nor the human will conscious,
Holy is lucidity
And the mind that dare explain.

THE MARGINAL FIELD

On the chalk cliff edge struggles the final field
Of barley smutted with tares and marbled
With veins of rusted poppy as though the plough had
                              bled.
The sun is drowned in bird-wailing mist,
The sea and sky meet outside distinction
The landscape glares and stares—white poverty
Of gaslight diffused through frosted glass.

This field was the farmer's extremest thought
And its flinty heart became his heart
When he drove below the return it yields
The wage of the labourer sheeted in sweat.
Here the price and the cost cross on a chart
At a point fixed on the margin of profit
Which opens out in the golden fields

Waving their grasses and virile beards
On the laps of the dripping valleys and flushing
Their pulsing ears against negative skies.
Their roots clutch into the flesh of the soil,
As they fall to the scythe they whisper of excess
Heaped high above the flat wavering scale
Near the sea, beyond the wind-scarred hill

Where loss is exactly equalled by gain
And the roots and the sinews wrestle with stone
On the margin of what can just be done
To eat back from the land the man the land eats.
Starved outpost of wealth and final soldier,
Your stretched-out bones are the frontier of power.
With your mouth wide open to drink in lead.

FALL OF A CITY

All the posters on the walls
All the leaflets in the streets
Are mutilated, destroyed or run in rain,
Their words blotted out with tears,
Skins peeling from their bodies
In the victorious hurricane.

All the names of heroes in the hall
Where the feet thundered and the bronze throats roared,
Fox and Lorca claimed as history on the walls,
Are now argrily deleted
Or to dust surrender their dust,
From golden praise excluded.

All the badges and salutes
Torn from lapels and from hands
Are thrown away with human sacks they wore
Or in the deepest bed of mind
They are washed over with a smile
Which launches the victors when they win.

All the lessons learned, unlearnt;
The young, who learned to read, now blind
Their eyes with an archaic film;
The peasant relapses to a stumbling tune
Following the donkey's bray;
These only remember to forget.

But somewhere some word presses
On the high door of a skull, and in some corner
Of an irrefrangible eye
Some old man's memory jumps to a child
—Spark from the days of energy.
And the child hoards it like a bitter toy.

WINTER AND SUMMER

Within my head, aches the perpetual winter
Of this violent time, where pleasures freeze.
My inner eye anticipates for ever
Looking through naked trees and running wheels
Onto a blank transparent sky
Leading to nothing; as though, through iron aims,
It was stared back at by filmy surface
Of a lid covering its own despair.
Thus, when the summer breaks upon my face
With the outward shock of a green wave
Crested with leaves and creamy foam of flowers,
I think the luxurious lazy meadows
Are a deceiving canvas covering
With a balmy paint of leafy billows,

The furious volleys of charioteering power
Behind the sun, racing to destroy.
   When under light lawns, heavy in their soil,
I hear the groaning of the wasted lives
Of those who revolve unreflecting wheels,
   Alas, I prove that I am right,
For if my shadowed mind affirmed the light
It would return to those green, foolish years
When to live seemed to stand knee-deep in flowers:
There, winter was an indoor accident,
Where, with head pressed against the glass, I watched
The garden, falsified by snow,
Waiting to melt, and become real again.

THE BARN

   Half-hidden by trees, the sheer roof of the barn
   Is warped to a river of tiles
   By currents of the sky's weather
   Through long damp years.

   Under the leaves, a great butterfly's wing
   Seems its brilliant red, streaked with dark lines
   Of lichen and rust, an underwing
   Of winter leaves.

   A sapling, with a jet of flaming
   Foliage, cancels with its branches
   The guttered lower base of the roof, reflecting
   The tiles in a cup of green.

Under the crashing vault of sky,
At the side of the road flashing past
With a rumour of smoke and steel,
Hushed by whispers of leaves, and bird song,
The barn from its dark throat
Gurgitates with a gentle booming murmur.

This ghost of a noise suggests a gust
Caught in its rafters aloft long ago,
The turn of a winch, the wood of a wheel.

Tangled in the sound, as in a girl's hair
Is the enthusiastic scent
Of vivid yellow straw, lit by a sun-beam
Laden with motes, on the boards of a floor.

DAYBREAK

At dawn she lay with her profile at that angle
Which, sleeping, seems the stone face of an angel;
Her hair a harp the hand of a breeze follows
To play, against the white cloud of the pillows.
Then in a flush of rose she woke, and her eyes were open
Swimming with blue through the rose flesh of dawn.
From her dew of lips, the drop of one word
Fell, from a dawn of fountains, when she murmured
"Darling",—upon my heart the song of the first bird.
"My dream glides in my dream", she said, "come true.
I waken from you to my dream of you."
O, then my waking dream dared to assume
The audacity of her sleep. Our dreams
Flowed into each other's arms, like streams.

LOUIS MACNEICE

BIRMINGHAM

Smoke from the train-gulf hid by hoardings blunders
             upward, the brakes of cars
Pipe as the policeman pivoting round raises his flat
             hand, bars
With his figure of a monolith Pharaoh the queue of
             fidgety machines
(Chromium dogs on the bonnet, faces behind the triplex
             screens),
Behind him the streets run away between the proud glass
             of shops,
Cubical scent-bottles artificial legs arctic foxes and
             electric mops,
But beyond this centre the slumward vista thins like a
             diagram:
There, unvisited, are Vulcan's forges who doesn't care a
             tinker's damn.

Splayed outwards through the suburbs houses, houses for
             rest
Seducingly rigged by the builder, half-timbered houses
             with lips pressed

So tightly and eyes staring at the traffic through bleary
haws
And only a six-inch grip of the racing earth in their
concrete claws;
In these houses men as in a dream pursue the Platonic
Forms
With wireless and cairn terriers and gadgets approximat-
ing to the fickle norms
And endeavour to find God and score one over the
neighbour
By climbing tentatively upward on jerry-built beauty
and sweated labour.

The lunch hour: the shops empty, shopgirls' faces relax
Diaphanous as green glass, empty as old almanacs
As incoherent with ticketed gewgaws tiered behind their
heads
As the Burne-Jones windows in St. Philip's broken by
crawling leads
Insipid colour, patches of emotion, Saturday thrills
(This theatre is sprayed with 'June')—the gutter take our
old playbills,
Next week-end it is likely in the heart's funfair we shall
pull
Strong enough on the handle to get back our money; or at
any rate it is possible.

On shining lines the trams like vast sarcophagi move
Into the sky, plum after sunset, merging to duck's egg,
barred with mauve

Zeppelin clouds, and Pentecost-like the cars' headlights
                                                bud
Out from sideroads and the trafic signals, crême-de-
                                            menthe or bull's blood,
Tell one to stop, the engine gently breathing, or to go on
To where like black pipes of organs in the frayed and
                                            fading zone
Of the West the factory chimneys on sullen sentry will
                                            all night wait
To call, in the harsh morning, sleep-stupid faces through
                                            the daily gate.

SNOW

The room was suddenly rich and the great bay-window
                                                was
Spawning snow and pink roses against it
Soundlessly collateral and incompatible:
World is suddener than we fancy it.

World is crazier and more of it than we think,
Incorrigibly plural. I peel and portion
A tangerine and spit the pips and feel
The drunkenness of things being various.

And the fire flames with a bubbling sound for world
Is more spiteful and gay than one supposes—
On the tongue on the eyes on the ears in the palms of
                                            one's hands—
There is more than glass between the snow and the huge
                                            roses.

"SLEEP, MY BODY, SLEEP, MY GHOST"

Sleep, my body, sleep, my ghost,
  Sleep, my parents and grand-parents,
And all those I have loved most:
  One man's coffin is another's cradle.
Sleep, my past and all my sins,
  In distant snow or dried roses
Under the moon for night's cocoon will open
  When day begins.
Sleep, my fathers, in your graves
  On upland bogland under heather;
What the wind scatters the wind saves,
  A sapling springs in a new country.
Time is a country, the present moment
  A spotlight roving round the scene;
We need not chase the spotlight,
  The future is the bride of what has been.
Sleep, my fancies and my wishes,
  Sleep a little and wake strong,
The same but different and take my blessing—
  A cradle-song.
And sleep, my various and conflicting
  Selves I have so long endured,
Sleep in Asclepius' temple
  And wake cured.
And you with whom I shared an idyll
  Five years long,
Sleep beyond the Atlantic
  And wake to a glitter of dew and to bird-song.

And you whose eyes are blue, whose ways are foam,
  Sleep quiet and smiling
And do not hanker
  For a perfection which can never come.
And you whose minutes patter
  To crowd the social hours,
Curl up easy in a placid corner
  And let your thoughts close in like flowers.
And you, who work for Christ, and you, as eager
  For a better life, humanist, atheist,
And you, devoted to a cause, and you, to a family,
  Sleep and may your beliefs and zeal persist.
Sleep quietly, Marx and Freud,
  The figure-heads of our transition.
Cagney, Lombard, Bing and Garbo,
  Sleep in your world of celluloid.
Sleep now also, monk and satyr,
  Cease your wrangling for a night.
Sleep, my brain, and sleep, my senses,
  Sleep, my hunger and my spite.
Sleep, recruits to the evil army,
  Who, for so long misunderstood,
Took to the gun to kill your sorrow;
  Sleep and be damned and wake up good.
While we sleep, what shall we dream?
  Of Tir nan Og or South Sea islands,
Of a land where all the milk is cream
  And all the girls are willing?
Or shall our dream be earnest of the real
  Future when we wake,
Design a home, a factory, a fortress

Which, though with effort, we can really make?
What is it we want really?
   For what end and how?
If it is something feasible, obtainable,
   Let us dream it now,
And pray for a possible land
   Not of sleep-walkers, not of angry puppets,
But where both heart and brain can understand
   The movements of our fellows;
Where life is a choice of instruments and none
   Is debarred his natural music,
Where the waters of life are free of the ice-blockade of
                                    hunger
   And thought is free as the sun,
Where the altars of sheer power and mere profit
   Have fallen to disuse,
Where nobody sees the use
   Of buying money and blood at the cost of blood and
                                    money,
Where the individual, no longer squandered
   In self-assertion, works with the rest, endowed
With the split vision of a juggler and the quick lock of a
                                    taxi,
   Where the people are more than a crowd.
So sleep in hope of this—but only for a little;
   Your hope must wake
While the choice is yours to make,
   The mortgage not foreclosed, the offer open.
Sleep serene, avoid the backward
   Glance; go forward, dreams, and do not halt
(Behind you in the desert stands a token

Of doubt—a pillar of salt).
Sleep, the past, and wake, the future,
   And walk out promptly through the open door;
But you, my coward doubts, may go on sleeping,
   You need not wake again—not any more.
The New Year comes with bombs, it is too late
   To dose the dead with honourable intentions:
If you have honour to spare, employ it on the living;
   The dead are dead as 1938.
Sleep to the noise of running water
   To-morrow to be crossed, however deep;
This is no river of the dead or Lethe,
   To-night we sleep
On the banks of Rubicon—the die is cast;
   There will be time to audit
The accounts later, there will be sunlight later
   And the equation will come out at last.

CUSHENDUN

Fuchsia and ragweed and the distant hills
Made as it were out of clouds and sea:
All night the bay is plashing and the moon
   Marks the break of the waves.

Limestone and basalt and a whitewashed house
With passages of great stone flags
And a walled garden with plums on the wall
   And a bird piping in the night.

Forgetfulness: brass lamps and copper jugs
And home-made bread and the smell of turf or flax
And the air a glove and the water lathering easy
   And convolvulus in the hedge.

Only in the dark green room beside the fire
With the curtains drawn against the winds and waves
There is a little box with a well-bred voice:
   What a place to talk of War.

COUNTY SLIGO

In Sligo the country was soft; there were turkeys
   Gobbling under sycamore trees
And the shadows of clouds on the mountains moving
   Like browsing cattle at ease.

And little distant fields were sprigged with haycocks
   And splashed against a white
Roadside cottage a welter of nasturtium
   Deluging the sight,

And pullets pecking the flies from around the eyes of
                            heifers
   Sitting in farmyard mud
Among hydrangeas and the falling ear-rings
   Of fuchsias red as blood.

But in Mayo the tumbledown walls went leap-frog
   Over the moors,

The sugar and salt in the pubs were damp in the casters
  And the water was brown as beer upon the shores

Of desolate loughs, and stumps of hoary bog-oak
  Stuck up here and there
And as the twilight filtered on the heather
  Water-music filled the air,

And when the night came down upon the bogland
  With all-enveloping wings
The coal-black turfstacks rose against the darkness
  Like the tombs of nameless kings.

ORDER TO VIEW

It was a big house, bleak;
Grass on the drive;
We had been there before
But memory, weak in front of
A blistered door, could find
Nothing alive now;
The shrubbery dripped, a crypt
Of leafmould dreams; a tarnished
Arrow over an empty stable
Shifted a little in the almost wind,

And wishes were unable
To rise; on the garden wall
The pear trees had come loose
From rotten loops; one wish,
A rainbow bubble, rose,

Faltered, broke in the dull
Air—What was the use?
The bell-pull would not pull
And the whole place, one might
Have supposed, was deadly ill:
The world was closed,

And remained closed until
A sudden angry tree
Shook itself like a setter
Flouncing out of a pond
And beyond the sombre line
Of limes a cavalcade
Of clouds rose like a shout of
Defiance. Near at hand
Somewhere in a loose-box
A horse neighed
And all the curtains flew out of
The windows; the world was open.

March, 1940

PROVENCE

It is a decade now since he and she
Spent September in Provence: the vineyard
Was close about the house; mosquitoes and cicadas
Garrulous day and night; and by the sea
Thighs and shoulders tanning themselves and one
Gay old man in particular who never
Missed a day, a glutton for the sun,
But did not bathe. He and she with swimming

Every noon were wild for food; a Basque
Woman cooked on charcoal—aubergine with garlic,
And there were long green grapes exploding on the palate
And smelling of eau de Cologne. They had nothing to ask
Except that it should go on. Watching the vintage—
A file of bullock carts and the muzzle of each
Animal munching purple—he suddenly said
'We must get married soon.' Down on the beach,
His wife and three of his three children dead,
An old man lay in the sun, perfectly happy.

September, 1940

DÉBÂCLE

They had built it up—but not for this the lean
And divinatory years,
The red-eyed pioneers
Facing the dark and making the desert green.

Not for this the pale inventor's lamp
Alight till dawn, the hands
Weary with sifting sands,
The burst of nuggets on the miner's camp.

Vision and sinew made it of light and stone;
Not grateful nor enchanted
Their heirs took it for granted
Having a world—a world that was all their own.

At sundown now the windows had gone gold
For half an hour; a quick

Chill came off the brick
Walls and the flesh was suddenly old and cold.

Crumbling between the fingers, under the feet,
Crumbling behind the eyes,
Their world gives way and dies
And something twangs and breaks at the end of the street.

September, 1940

EXILE

Now he can hardly press
The heavy pedals of thought,
Tired of what he wants
And sick of what he ought,
He is content to watch
The window fill with snow
Making even the Future
Seem long ago.

Knowing that in Europe
All the streets are black
And that stars of blood
Star the almanac,
One half-hour's reprieve
Drowns him in the white
Physical or spiritual
Inhuman night.

March, 1940

PRAYER BEFORE BIRTH

I am not yet born; O hear me.
Let not the bloodsucking bat or the rat or the stoat or the
    club-footed ghoul come near me.

I am not yet born, console me.
I fear that the human race may with tall walls wall me,
    with strong drugs dope me, with wise lies lure me,
        on black racks rack me, in blood-baths roll me.

I am not yet born; provide me
With water to dandle me, grass to grow for me, trees to
                        talk
    to me, sky to sing to me, birds and a white light
        in the back of my mind to guide me.

I am not yet born, forgive me
For the sins that in me the world shall commit, my words
    when they speak me, my thoughts when they think
                    me,
      my treason engendered by traitors beyond me,
        my life when they murder by means of my
        hands, my death when they live me.

I am not yet born; rehearse me
In the parts I must play and the cues I must take when
    old men lecture me, bureaucrats hector me, mountains
    frown at me, lovers laugh at me, the white

waves call me to folly and the desert calls
me to doom and the beggar refuses
my gift and my children curse me.

I am not yet born; O hear me,
Let not the man who is beast or who thinks he is God
come near me.

I am not yet born; O fill me
With strength against those who would freeze my
humanity, would dragoon me into a lethal automaton,
would make me a cog in a machine, a thing with
one face, a thing, and against all those
who would dissipate my entirety, would
blow me like thistledown hither and
thither or hither and thither
like water held in the
hands would spill me
Let them not make me a stone and let them not spill me.
Otherwise kill me.

WILLIAM EMPSON

THE SCALES

The proper scale would pat you on the head
But Alice showed her pup Ulysses' bough
Well from behind a thistle, wise with dread;

And though your gulf-sprung mountains I allow
(Snow-puppy curves, rose-solemn dado band)
Charming for nurse, I am not nurse just now.

Why pat or stride them, when the train will land
Me high, through climbing tunnels, at your side,
And careful fingers meet through castle sand.

Claim slyly rather that the tunnels hide
Solomon's gems, white vistas, preserved kings,
By jackal sandhole to your aim flung wide.

Say (she suspects) to sea Nile only brings
Delta and indecision, who instead
Far back up country does enormous things.

HOMAGE TO THE BRITISH MUSEUM

There is a supreme God in the ethnological section;
A hollow toad shape, faced with a blank shield.
He needs his belly to include the Pantheon,
Which is inserted through a hole behind.
At the navel, at the points formally stressed, at the organs
                                        of sense,
Lice glue themselves, dolls, local deities,
His smooth wood creeps with all the creeds of the
                                        world

Attending there let us absorb the cultures of nations
And dissolve into our judgement all their codes.
Then, being clogged with a natural hesitation
(People are continually asking one the way out),
Let us stand here and admit that we have no road.
Being everything, let ur admit that is to be something,
Or give ourselves the benefit of the doubt;
Let us offer our pinch of dust all to this God,
And grant his reign over the entire building.

AUBADE

Hours before dawn we were woken by the quake.
My house was on a cliff. The thing could take
Bookloads off shelves, break bottles in a row.
Then the long pause and then the bigger shake.
It seemed the best thing to be up and go.

And far too large for my feet to step by.
I hoped that various buildings were brought low.
The heart of standing is you cannot fly.

It seemed quite safe till she got up and dressed.
The guarded tourist makes the guide the test.
Then I said The Garden? Laughing she said No.
Taxi for her and for me healthy rest.
It seemed the best thing to be up and go.

The language problem but you have to try.
Some solid ground for lying could she show?
The heart of standing is you cannot fly.

None of these deaths were her point at all.
The thing was that being woken he would bawl
And finding her not in earshot he would know.
I tried saying Half an Hour to pay this call.
It seemed the best thing to be up and go.

I slept, and blank as that I would yet lie.
Till you have seen what a threat holds below,
The heart of standing is you cannot fly.

Tell me again about Europe and her pains,
Who's tortured by the drought, who by the rains.
Glut me with floods where only the swine can row
Who cuts his throat and let him count his gains.
It seemed the best thing to be up and go.

A bedshift flight to a Far Eastern sky.
Only the same war on a stronger toe.
The heart of standing is you cannot fly.

Tell me more quickly what I lost by this,
Or tell me with less drama what they miss
Who call no die a god for a good throw,
Who say after two aliens had one kiss
It seemed the best thing to be up and go.

But as to risings, I can tell you why.
It is on contradiction that they grow.
It seemed the best thing to be up and go.
Up was the heartening and the strong reply.
The heart of standing is we cannot fly.

REFLECTION FROM ROCHESTER

'But wretched Man is still in arms for Fear.'

'From fear to fear, successively betrayed'—
By making risks to give a cause for fear
(Feeling safe with causes, and from birth afraid),

By climbing higher not to look down, by mere
Destruction of the accustomed because strange
(Too complex a loved system, or too clear),

By needing change but not too great a change
And therefore a new fear—man has achieved
All the advantage of a wider range,

Successfully has the first fear deceived,
Thought the wheels run on sleepers. This is not
The law of nature it has been believed.

Increasing power (it has increased a lot)
Embarrasses 'attempted suicides',
Narrows their margin. Policies that got

'Virility from war' get much besides;
The mind, as well in mining as in gas
War's parallel, now less easily decides

On a good root-confusion to amass
Much safety from irrelevant despair.
Mere change in numbers made the process crass.

We now turn blank eyes for a pattern there
Where first the race of armament was made;
Where a less involute compulsion played.
'For hunger or for love they bite and tear.'

IGNORANCE OF DEATH

Then there is this civilising love of death, by which
Even music and painting tell you what else to love.
Buddhist and Christians contrive to agree about death

Making death their ideal basis for different ideals.
The communists however disapprove of death
Except when practical. The people who dig up

Corpses and rape them are I understand not reported.
The Freudians regard the death-wish as fundamental,
Though 'the clamour of life' proceeds from its rival 'Erol'.

Whether you are to admire a given case for making less
                                                        clamour
Is not their story. Liberal hopefulness
Regards death as a mere border to an improving picture.

Because we have neither hereditary nor direct knowledge
                                                        of death
It is the trigger of the literary man's biggest gun
And we are happy to equate it to any conceived calm.

Heaven me, when a man is ready to die about something
Other than himself, and is in fact ready because of that,
Not because of himself, that is something clear about
                                                        himself.

Otherwise I feel very blank upon this topic,
And think that though important, and proper for anyone
                                                        to bring up,
It is one that most people should be prepared to be blank
                                                        upon.

MISSING DATES

Slowly the poison the whole blood stream fills.
It is not the effort nor the failure tires.
The waste remains, the waste remains and kills.

It is not your system or clear sight that mills
Down small to the consequence a life requires;
Slowly the poison the whole blood stream fills.

They bled an old dog dry yet the exchange rills
Of young dog blood gave but a month's desires;
The waste remains, the waste remains and kills

It is the Chinese tombs and the slag hills
Usurp the soil, and not the soil retires.
Slowly the poison the whole blood stream fills.

Not to have fire is to be a skin that shrills.
The complete fire is death. From partial fires
The waste remains, the waste remains and kills

It is the poems you have lost, the ills
From missing dates, at which the heart expires
Slowly the poison the whole blood stream fills
The waste remains, the waste remains and kills

MANCHOULI

I find it normal, passing these great frontiers,
That you scan the crowds in rags eagerly each side
With awe; that the nations seem real; that their ambitions
Having such achieved variety within one type, seem sane;
I find it normal;
So too to extract false comfort from that word.

CHINA

The dragon hatched a cockatrice
   Cheese crumbles and not many mites repair
There is a Nature about this
   The spring and rawness tantalise the air

Most proud of being most at ease
   The sea is the most solid ground
Where comfort is on hands and knees
   The nations perch about around

Red hills bleed naked into screes—
   The classics are a single school
—The few large trees are holy trees
   They teach the nations how to rule

They will not teach the Japanese—
   They rule by music and by rites
—They are as like them as two peas
   All nations are untidy sights

The serious music strains to squeeze—
   The angel coolies sing like us
—Duties, and literature, and fees
   To lift an under-roaded bus

The paddy fields are wings of bees
   The Great Wall as a dragon crawls
To one who flies or one who sees
   The twisted contour of their walls

A liver fluke of sheep agrees
  Most rightly proud of her complacencies
With snail so well they make one piece
  Most wrecked and longest of all histories.

RONALD BOTTRALL

A GRAVE REVISITED

These we are given last to outstay farewells
And hand wringings, at the death when we ask for
Wing-folded peace and eddies of silence:
The madness of thick, clotted words,
The belly-piercing shriek of the tropical kingfisher,
The monotonous tock-tock of the brain-fever bird.
After this final pain earth stops the sensitive ear
No less firmly than the grossened membrane,
And weight of stone and tree lies as lightly
On the singer as on the dumb. But death levels
Only by deprivation; and lack of the familiar
Accent, of the accustomed carriage of the head,
Brings us back from halo and harp
To dust, to horizons of senseless rocks
And what the sea sifts and rejects, corpses,
The white isolation of local stone-bound graves.

In the winter's bud is furled summer's flower,
The condor's wing-spread is inherent
In the egg, and in the lineaments
Of the new-born child is felt the exquisite
Pressure of the past. Dead bodies have power

To fertilize; and what fashion of fruit
The grave has in store will be revealed at the ripe hour.
The moment may come in unexpected latitudes,
But let us watch that the posture is not unprepared
And the eye unsighted. There may be no sudden
Vision, no frenzied glory of victory or defeat,
Yet let not the axe descend until the guide-lines
Are established, until the oxen have been set
To the plough and the furrow laid open to the seed.

TWILIGHT GODS

The red that spattered yesterday's neat sunset
Will serve again to fret the morning heaven,
But pierce the heart with never so careful lancet
And ask in vain for what is not twice given.
Skies threshed by hailing wings, the musketry
That starts long ravels in the sleeve of summer,
Prelude gas-mottled eyes, and men that lie
Goughing in tune with a machine-gun stammer.

But time brings on his penalties unawares.
Our pilot pawn sickens in mid-endeavour
To flatten out his tailspin of lean years;
Unfriended, fever-ridden he dully hears
Whining cross-currents sound his zero hour.

Bondsmen exalt, to challenge our disclaimer,
The trophies of an ageing paradise,
Make stones, flowers, fountains in prime order witness
That rod and axe will call up a redeemer.

Newly enacted we hear Leda's swan-song
The tripping cackle of a slumming hostess
And watch her egg hatch out a cockatrice.
Spent overtones of a barbaric gong
Shatter no irons, tongue us no redress;
Bent heart re-forged alone has power to sing
Of the green light that rockets out with spring.

GENESIS

The child quickens the coy light of a candle
With faint voices and echoing alleys,
Fathers a world in nooks, thoroughfares in an angle.
But we have lost the transmuting eye that sees
Heaven in a sapphire light, or in a seared face hell.

The fisherman gleaming with salt pilchard scales,
Blackcocks burring on the wing, are taken
From our blood, and slatted prison walls
Fracture the fringes of our winter sun.

Time was, in the days of pilgrimage,
When the equinox leapt as a ram, green
As an emerald at the moment of its cleavage,
When the word ran rippling in a rune.

Now, constricted in an agony of labour
We retch our hearts out, teasing the sublime
To intricate motives, adequate to the hour,
And envy no man's pedestal of rhyme.

But the desert moth waits, dormant for years, to fertilize
The yucca blossom on its one night of flower,
And the listener patient with attuned ear
Will catch, at length, in the dead house infant cries.

FULFILMENT IS NOT IN WAITING

Seven long springs together we listened
Ears to earth for the growing of the daisy eyes
For the fructifying turnings of the worm,
And there was no sound:

Seven long summers we watched for the rains
Clouds coming over the horizon as big as a man's hand,
But there was a rustle of dry chaff
And the clanging of the cymbals of the prophets of Baal:

Seven long autumns we waited for the peach,
The nectarine, the bramble heavy with blackberries,
And our mouths were filled with the rotten seeds
Of sleepy pears:

Seven long winters we prayed for snow
To cover the hollows and ridges
Of the terrain with white equity,
And there were broken edges.

Drying and dying and trying to find speech,
How long have I sat waiting for the mountain stream
To cut the pebbles cleanly,
And it is the tepid, garrulous tide
Dispersing over the mud-flats that has come.

I am not asking for the incredible deftness of the spider
Or the adaptability of the chameleon
Or the ingenuity of the opossum
Or the fertility of the guinea-pig;
For me would suffice the surprise
Of the ordinary daily contact of lip with lip
And spirit with spirit.

DEFINITION OF LOVE

When love comes there should be
Quick indrawn breath at the sight of a head-turn
Or the apprehension of a slight quiver
Of an eyelid. Then the apertures of sense
Stretch themselves to absorb
Experiences hitherto unsought, tintinnabulations
Of heart distantly calling to heart, the curb
And cold of unexpected absence,
The soothing profile of warm return.
Tension where there is feeling,
A taut rope over precipices
And the distant thunder of cataracts of tears,
Is preferable to the interminable spaces
Without landmarks, without trees, without rivers.
When a polite company is visiting the theatre
The extent of the lethargy and the horror
Stretched between man and woman
Is not to be gauged by the pity and terror
Expelled and compensated by the action on the stage,
But rather by the diminuendos

Of the conversation between the acts.
Love is something winged
And on fire, bridging gulfs, squaring
Circles, transmuting commonplaces,
Challenging impossibilities.
This may be the wild talk of a lover
But this is what we are discussing now, love.
It may come when least asked-for,
Be withheld to the most piteous prayers,
Come stealing in the night
Or rushing as an express train
Assaults the eye in the cinema.
But when it comes it cannot be mistaken.
About its endurance no one can boast
Without foolhardiness, but of its possession
One can speak with confidence and pride.
It is not something to be mewed in corners
But to be bruited to the world in market places;
It does not need the artificiality
Of loud-speakers or the bravado of advertisement,
But it penetrates to the inmost recesses
Nor does it fear the light of day.
Love can be measured only with divine scales
Not by the pennyweight standard of the provincial grocer
Or the proprieties of a Kensington drawing-room.
Love is not round the corner or left in the nursery,
Or seen on Broadway or pictured in Bali,
It is here and now, or never.
It is pervasive in the sick-bed, the tenement,
The lathe, the scalpel, the microscope,
It permeates the ganglia and the chromosomes;

It is proud in the border of high sunflowers
And meek with the crouching violet.
Praise.

NEW BOUNDARIES

Practice of love makes perfect
The fraction of desire
And floods the passionate object
With cool fire.

The war of give and take
Expires in sacrifice;
Amorphous and opaque
Crystallize.

The specious ways of wounds
Are cauterized with smiles
And jealousy's beaten hounds
Cower in defiles.

Great love contains the less
And pity self-pity quells,
As world-pain on the cross
Drove out the nails.

Assumption of delight
Heightens what flesh has known
And radiates a new light
Through the world of bone.

MOVING DEPTHS

It may be asked what love has learned by knocking at
                              the door
With torn hands and bleeding nails, by pacing palisades
And probing darkness for a touch or word or tear
To tear the mask that cajoled a thousand trivial aubades.

Love, giving and waiting, extorts more fundamental
                              promises
Than passion that draws and drains and lives outside
                              itself.
It is not saying yes or no that ratifies a pact, or pieces
The intricate edges into a solid square to solve and salve.

Presume not to incriminate the slow equal growth
Of lilies clothing a pond, by crying for the mountain race
Bucking with foam. Beneath the face of enamelled sloth
Quivering life breaks from capsule and sheath into light-
                              winged, dragonish grace.

DAPHNE

She ran, romp of a race, head over trace,
Back glancing, with the doubt of a quarter-miler
In echelon, at the terror and grace
Of the gaining god, bent to enwile her
Fresh, virginal as a reed. As she skimmed the earth
She felt the pressure of her mother's flesh
Expelling her in a rhythmic pang forth
To hazard the tender trauma of light's flush

Flowers were her ears, her finger-nails sprouted
In tendrils, and her arms were soothed in sleeves
Of bark watered by rain-filled eyes, enrooted
Her feet, her thought vegetable as sheaves
Of corn; on her branching limbs birds footed
While divine music rustled through her leaves.

DYLAN THOMAS

"THE FORCE THAT THROUGH THE GREEN FUSE DRIVES THE FLOWER"

The force that through the green fuse drives the flower
Drives my green age; that blasts the roots of trees
Is my destroyer.
And I am dumb to tell the crooked rose
My youth is bent by the same wintry fever.

The force that drives the water through the rocks
Drives my red blood; that dries the mouthing streams
Turns mine to wax.
And I am dumb to mouth unto my veins
How at the mountain spring the same mouth sucks.

The hand that whirls the water in the pool
Stirs the quicksand; that ropes the blowing wind
Hauls my shroud sail.
And I am dumb to tell the hanging man
How of my clay is made the hangman's lime.

The lips of time leech to the fountain head;
Love drips and gathers, but the fallen blood
Shall calm her sores.

And I am dumb to tell a weather's wind
How time has ticked a heaven round the stars.

And I am dumb to tell the lover's tomb
How at my sheet goes the same crooked worm.

"WHERE ONCE THE WATERS"

Where once the waters of your face
Spun to my screws, your dry ghost blows,
The dead turns up its eye;
Where once the mermen through your ice
Pushed up their hair, the dry wind steers
Through salt and root and roe.

Where once your green knots sank their splice
Into the tided cord, there goes
The green unraveller,
His scissors oiled, his knife hung loose
To cut the channels at their source
And lay the wet fruits low.

Invisible, your clocking tides
Break on the lovebeds of the weeds;
The weed of love's left dry;
There round about your stones the shades
Of children go who, from their voids,
Cry to the dolphined sea.

Dry as a tomb, your coloured lids
Shall not be latched while magic glides

Sage on the earth and sky;
There shall be corals in your beds,
There shall be serpents in your tides,
Till all our sea-faiths die.

"OUR EUNUCH DREAMS"

Our eunuch dreams, all seedless in the light,
Of light and love, the tempers of the heart,
Whack their boy's limbs,
And, winding-footed in their shawl and sheet,
Groom the dark brides, the widows of the night
Fold in their arms.

The shades of girls, all flavoured from their shrouds,
When sunlight goes are sundered from the worm,
The bones of men, the broken in their beds,
By midnight pulleys that unhouse the tomb.

"ESPECIALLY WHEN THE OCTOBER WIND"

Especially when the October wind
With frosty fingers punishes my hair,
Caught by the crabbing sun I walk on fire
And cast a shadow crab upon the land,
By the sea's side, hearing the noise of birds,
Hearing the raven cough in winter sticks,
My busy heart who shudders as she talks
Sheds the syllabic blood and drains her words.

Shut, too, in a tower of words, I mark
On the horizon walking like the trees
The wordy shapes of women, and the rows
Of the star-gestured children in the park.
Some let me make you of the vowelled beeches,
Some of the oaken voices, from the roots
Of many a thorny shire tell you notes,
Some let me make you of the water's speeches.

Behind a pot of ferns the wagging clock
Tells me the hour's word, the neural meaning
Flies on the shafted disc, declaims the morning
And tells the windy weather in the cock.
Some let me make you of the meadow's signs;
The signal grass that tells me all I know
Breaks with the wormy winter through the eye.
Some let me tell you of the raven's sins.

Especially when the October wind
(Some let me make you of autumnal spells,
The spider-tongued, and the loud hill of Wales)
With fist of turnips punishes the land,
Some let me make you of the heartless words.
The heart is drained that, spelling in the scurry
Of chemic blood, warned of the coming fury.
By the sea's side hear the dark-vowelled birds.

"I, IN MY INTRICATE IMAGE"

I

I, in my intricate image, stride on two levels,
Forged in man's minerals, the brassy orator
Laying my ghost in metal,
The scales of this twin world tread on the double,
My half ghost in armour hold hard in death's corridor,
To my man-iron sidle.

Beginning with doom in the bulb, the spring unravels,
Bright as her spinning-wheels, the colic season
Worked on a world of petals;
She threads off the sap and needles, blood and bubble
Casts to the pine roots, raising man like a mountain
Out of the naked entrail.

Beginning with doom in the ghost, and the springing
marvels,
Image of images, my metal phantom
Forcing forth through the harebell,
My man of leaves and the bronze root, mortal, unmortal,
I, in my fusion of rose and male motion,
Create this twin miracle.

This is the fortune of manhood: the natural peril,
A steeplejack tower, bonerailed and masterless,
No death more natural;
Thus the shadowless man or ox, and the pictured devil,
In seizure of silence commit the dead nuisance:
The natural parallel.

My images stalk the trees and the slant sap's tunnel,
No tread more perilous, the green steps and spire
Mount on man's footfall,
I with the wooden insect in the tree of nettles,
In the glass bed of grapes with snail and flower,
Hearing the weather fall.

Intricate manhood of ending, the invalid rivals,
Voyaging clockwise off the symboled harbour,
Finding the water final,
On the consumptives' terrace taking their two farewells,
Sail on the level, the departing adventure,
To the sea-blown arrival.

II

They climb the country pinnacle,
Twelve winds encounter by the white host at pasture,
Corner the mounted meadows in the hill corral;
They see the squirrel stumble,
The haring snail go giddily round the flower,
A quarrel of weathers and trees in the windy spiral.

As they dive, the dust settles,
The cadaverous gravels, falls thick and steadily,
The highroad of water where the seabear and mackerel
Turn the long sea arterial
Turning a petrol face blind to the enemy
Turning the riderless dead by the channel wall.

(Death instrumental,
Splitting the long eye open, and the spiral turnkey,
Your corkscrew grave centred in navel and nipple,
The neck of the nostril,
Under the mask and the ether, they making bloody
The tray of knives, the antiseptic funeral;

Bring out the black patrol,
Your monstrous officers and the decaying army,
The sexton sentinel, garrisoned under thistles,
A cock-on-a-dunghill
Crowing to Lazarus the morning is vanity,
Dust be your saviour under the conjured soil.)

As they drown, the chime travels,
Sweetly the diver's bell in the steeple of spindrift
Rings out the Dead Sea scale;
And, clapped in water till the triton dangles,
Strung by the flaxen whale-weed, from the hangman's
                                                raft,
Hear they the salt glass breakers and the tongues of
                                                burial.

(Turn the sea-spindle lateral,
The grooved land rotating, that the stylus of lightning
Dazzle this face of voices on the moon-turned table,
Let the wax disc babble
Shames and the damp dishonours, the relic scraping.
These are your years' recorders. The circular world
                                                stands still.)

III

They suffer the undead water where the turtle nibbles,
Come unto sea-stuck towers, at the fibre scaling,
The flight of the carnal skull
And the cell-stepped thimble;
Suffer, my topsy-turvies, that a double angel
Sprout from the stony lockers like a tree on Aran.

Be by your one ghost pierced, his pointed ferrule,
Brass and the bodiless image, on a stick of folly
Star-set at Jacob's angle,
Smoke hill and hophead's valley,
And the five-fathomed Hamlet on his father's coral,
Thrusting the tom-thumb vision up the iron mile.

Suffer the slash of vision by the fin-green stubble,
Be by the ships' sea broken at the manstring anchored
The stoved bones' voyage downward
In the shipwreck of muscle;
Give over, lovers, locking, and the seawax struggle,
Love like a mist or fire through the bed of eels.

And in the pincers of the boiling circle,
The sea and instrument, nicked in the locks of time,
My great blood's iron single
In the pouring town,
I, in a wind on fire, from green Adam's cradle,
No man more magical, clawed out the crocodile.

Man was the scales, the death birds on enamel,
Tail, Nile, and snout, a saddler of the rushes,
Time in the hourless houses
Shaking the sea-hatched skull,
And, as for oils and ointments on the flying grail,
All-hollowed man wept for his white apparel.

Man was Cadaver's masker, the harnessing mantle,
Windily master of man was the rotten fathom,
My ghost in his metal neptune
Forged in man's mineral.
This was the god of beginning in the intricate seawhirl,
And my images roared and rose on heaven's hill.

"HOLD HARD, THESE ANCIENT MINUTES"

Hold hard, these ancient minutes in the cuckoo's month,
Under the lank, fourth folly on Glamorgan's hill,
As the green blooms ride upward, to the drive of time;
Time, in a folly's rider, like a county man
Over the vault of ridings with his hound at heel,
Drives forth my men, my children, from the hanging
                                                    south.

Country, your sport is summer, and December's pools
By crane and water-tower by the seedy trees
Lie this fifth month unskated, and the birds have flown;
Hold hard, my country children in the world of tales,
The greenwood dying as the deer fall in their tracks,
This first and steepled season, to the summer's game.

And now the horns of England, in the sound of shape,
Summon your snowy horsemen, and the four-stringed hill,
Over the sea-gut loudening, sets a rock alive;
Hurdles and guns and railings, as the boulders heave,
Crack like a spring in a vice, bone breaking April,
Spill the lank folly's hunter and the hard-held hope.

Down fall four padding weathers on the scarlet lands,
Stalking my children's faces with a tail of blood,
Time, in a rider rising, from the harnessed valley;
Hold hard, my county darlings, for a hawk descends,
Golden Glamorgan straightens, to the falling birds.
Your sport is summer as the spring runs angrily.

"WAS THERE A TIME"

Was there a time when dancers with their fiddles
In children's circuses could stay their troubles?
There was a time they could cry over books,
But time has set its maggot on their track.
Under the arc of the sky they are unsafe.
What's never known is safest in this life.
Under the skysigns they who have no arms
Have cleanest hands, and, as the heartless ghost
Alone's unhurt, so the blind man sees best.

"AND DEATH SHALL HAVE NO DOMINION"

And death shall have no dominion.
Dead men naked they shall be one
With the man in the wind and the west moon;

When their bones are picked clean and the clean bones
gone,
They shall have stars at elbow and foot;
Though they go mad they shall be sane,
Though they sink through the sea they shall rise again;
Though lovers be lost love shall not;
And death shall have no dominion.

And death shall have no dominion.
Under the windings of the sea
They lying long shall not die windily;
Twisting on racks when sinews give way,
Strapped to a wheel, yet they shall not break;
Faith in their hands shall snap in two,
And the unicorn evils run them through;
Split all ends up they shan't crack;
And death shall have no dominion.

And death shall have no dominion.
No more may gulls cry at their ears
Or waves break loud on the seashores;
Where blew a flower may a flower no more
Lift its head to the blows of the rain;
Though they be mad and dead as nails,
Heads of the characters hammer through daisies;
Break in the sun till the sun breaks down,
And death shall have no dominion.

"NOW STAMP THE LORD'S PRAYER"

Now stamp the Lord's Prayer on a grain of rice,
A Bible-leaved of all the written woods

Strip to this tree: a rocking alphabet,
Genesis in the root, the scarecrow word,
And one light's language in the book of trees;
Doom on deniers at the wind-turned statement.
Time's tune my ladies with the teats of music,
The scaled sea-sawers, fix in a naked sponge
Who sucks the bell-voiced Adam out of magic,
Time, milk, and magic, from the world beginning.
Time is the tune my ladies lend their heartbreak,
From bald pavilions and the house of bread
Time tracks the sound of shape on man and cloud,
On rose and icicle the ringing handprint.

"FROM THE ORACULAR ARCHIVES"

From the oracular archives and the parchment,
Prophets and fibre kings in oil and letter,
The lamped calligrapher, the queen in splints,
Buckle to lint and cloth their natron footsteps,
Draw on the glove of prints, dead Cairo's henna
Pour like a halo on the caps and serpents.
This was the resurrection in the desert,
Death from a bandage, rants the mask of scholars
Gold on such features, and the linen spirit
Weds my long gentleman to dusts and furies;
With priest and pharaoh bed my gentle wound,
World in the sand, on the triangle landscape,
With stones of odyssey for ash and garland
And rivers of the dead around my neck.

IN MEMORY OF ANN JONES

After the funeral, mule praises, brays,
Windshake of sailshaped ears, muffle-toed tap
Tap happily of one peg in the thick
Grave's foot, blinds down the lids, the teeth in black,
The spittled eyes, the salt ponds in the sleeves,
Morning smack of the spade that wakes up sleep,
Shakes a desolate boy who slits his throat
In the dark of the coffin and sheds dry leaves,
That breaks one bone to light with a judgment clout,
After the feast of tear-stuffed time and thistles
In a room with a stuffed fox and a stale fern,
I stand, for this memorial's sake, alone
In the snivelling hours with dead, humped Ann
Whose hooded, fountain heart once fell in puddles
Round the parched worlds of Wales and drowned each
                                    sun
(Though this for her is a monstrous image blindly
Magnified out of praise; her death was a still drop;
She would not have me sinking in the holy
Flood of her heart's fame; she would lie dumb and deep
And need no druid of her broken body).
But I, Ann's bard on a raised hearth, call all
The seas to service that her wood-tongued virtue
Babble like a bellbuoy over the hymning heads,
Bow down the walls of the ferned and foxy woods
That her love sing and swing through a brown chapel,
Bless her bent spirit with four, crossing birds.
Her flesh was meek as milk, but this skyward statue
With the wild breast and blessed and giant skull

Is carved from her in a room with a wet window
In a fiercely mourning house in a crooked year.
I know her scrubbed and sour humble hands
Lie with religion in their cramp, her threadbare
Whisper in a damp word, her wits drilled hollow,
Her fist of a face died clenched on a round pain;
And sculptured Ann is seventy years of stone.
These cloud-sopped, marble hands, this monumental
Argument of the hewn voice, gesture and psalm
Storm me forever over her grave until
The stuffed lung of the fox twitch and cry Love
And the strutting fern lay seeds on the black sill.

"THE TOMBSTONE TOLD WHEN SHE DIED"

The tombstone told when she died.
Her two surnames stopped me still.
A virgin married at rest.
She married in this pouring place,
That I struck one day by luck,
Before I heard in my mother's side
Or saw in the looking-glass shell
The rain through her cold heart speak
And the sun killed in her face.
More the thick stone cannot tell.

Before she lay on a stranger's bed
With a hand plunged through her hair,
Or that rainy tongue beat back
Through the devilish years and innocent deaths

To the room of a secret child,
Among men later I heard it said
She cried her white-dressed limbs were bare
And her red lips where kissed black,
She wept in her pain and made mouths,
Talked and tore though her eyes smiled.

I who saw in a hurried film
Death and this mad heroine
Meet once on a mortal wall
Heard her speak through the chipped beak
Of the stone bird guarding her:
I died before bedtime came
But my womb was bellowing
And I felt with my bare fall
A blazing red harsh head tear up
And the dear floods of his hair.

"A SAINT ABOUT TO FALL"

A saint about to fall,
The stained flats of heaven hit and razed
To the kissed kite hems of his shawl,
On the last street wave praised
The unwinding, song by rock,
Of the woven wall
Of his father's house in the sands,
The vanishing of the musical ship-work and the chucked
                                    bells,
The wound-down cough of the blood-counting clock

Behind a face of hands,
On the angelic etna of the last whirring featherlands,
Wind-heeled foot in the hole of a fireball,
Hymned his shrivelling flock,
On the last rick's tip by spilled wine-wells
Sang heaven hungry and the quick
Cut Christbread spitting vinegar and all
The mazes of his praise and envious tongue were worked
                              in flames and shells.

Glory cracked like a flea.
The sun-leaved holy candlewoods
Drivelled down to one singeing tree
With a stub of black buds,
The sweet, fish-gilled boats bringing blood
Lurched through a scuttled sea
With a hold of leeches and straws,
Heaven fell with his fall and one crocked bell beat
                              the left air.
O wake in me in my house in the mud
Of the crotch of the squawking shores,
Flicked from the carbolic city puzzle in a bed of sores
The scudding base of the familiar sky,
The lofty roots of the clouds.
From an odd room in a split house stare,
Milk in your mouth, at the sour floods
That bury the sweet street slowly, see
The skull of the earth is barbed with a war of burning
                              brains and hair.

Strike in the time-bomb town,
Raise the live rafters of the eardrum,
Throw your fear a parcel of stone
Through the dark asylum,
Lapped among herods wail
As their blade marches in
That the eyes are already murdered,
The stocked heart is forced, and agony has another
                                        mouth to feed.
O wake to see, after a noble fall,
The old mud hatch again, the horrid
Woe drip from the dishrag hands and the pressed sponge
                                        of the forehead,
The breath draw back like a bolt through white oil
And a stranger enter like iron.
Cry joy that this witchlike midwife second
Bullies into rough seas you so gentle
And makes with a flick of the thumb and sun
A thundering bullring of your silent and girl-circled
                                        island.

"TWENTY-FOUR YEARS REMIND THE TEARS"

Twenty-four years remind the tears of my eyes.
(Bury the dead for fear that they walk to the grave
                                        in labour.)
In the groin of the natural doorway I crouched like
                                        a tailor
Sewing a shroud for a journey

By the light of the meat-eating sun.
Dressed to die, the sensual strut begun,
With my red veins full of money,
In the final direction of the elementary town
I advance for as long as forever is.

GEORGE BARKER

SUMMER IDYLL

Sometimes in summer months, the gestate earth
Loaded to gold, the boughs arching downward
Burdened, the shallow and glucose streams
Teeming, flowers out, all gold camouflage
Of the collusive summer; but under the streams
Winter lies coldly, and coldly embedded in
The corn hunger lies germinally, want under
The abundance, poverty pulling down
The tautened boughs, and need is the seed.

Robe them in superb summer, at angles
Their bones penetrate, or with a principality
Of Spring possess them, under the breast
Space of a vacancy spreads like a foul
Ghost flower, want; and the pressure upon
The eyeballs of their spirits, upon the organs
Of their spare bodies, the pressure upon
Their movement and their merriment, loving and
Living, the pressure upon their lives like deep
Seas, becomes insufferable, to be suffered.

Sometimes the summer lessens a moment the pressure.
Large as the summer rose some rise

Bathing in rivers or at evening harrying rabbits,
Indulging in games in meadows—and some are idle,
                                                    strewn
Over the parks like soiled paper like summer
Insects, bathed in sweat or at evening harried
By watchmen, park-keepers, policemen—indulge in
                                                    games
Dreaming as I dream of rest and cleanliness and cash.

And the gardens exhibit the regalia of the season
Like debutante queans, between which they wander
Blown with vague odours, seduced by the pure
Beauty, like drowned men floating in bright coral.
Summer, denuding young women, also denudes
Them, removes jackets, exposing backs—
Summer moves many up the river in boats

Trailing their fingers in the shadowed water; they
Too move by the river, and in the water shadows
Trail a hand, which need not find a bank,
Face downward like bad fruit. Cathedrals and Building
Societies, as they appear, disappear; and Beethoven
Is played more loudly to deafen the Welsh echoes,
And Summer, blowing over the Mediterranean
Like swans, like perfect swans.

"FROM THORAX OF STORMS THE VOICES OF VERBS"

From thorax of storms the voices of verbs
Shall call to me without sound, like the silence

Round which cyclones rage, to nurse my nerve
And hang my heart midway, where the balance
Meets. I taste sea swilling in my bowels
As I sit shivering in the swing of waves
Like a face in a bubble. As the hull heaves
I and my ghost tread water over hell.

The greedy bitch with sailors in her guts,
Green as a dream and formidable as God,
Spitting at stars, gnawing at shores, mad randy,
Riots with us on her abdomen and puts
Eternity in our cabins, pitches our pod
To the mouth of the death for which no one is ready.

"AND NOW THERE IS NOTHING LEFT TO CELEBRATE"

And now there is nothing left to celebrate
But the individual death in a ditch or a plane
Like a cock o'the north in a hurricane.
Out of the bogus glory and the synthetic hate,
The welter of nations and the speeches, O step down
You corpse in the gold and blue, out of a cloud,
My dragonfly, step down into your own:
The ditch and the dislocated wings and the cold
Kiss of the not to be monumental stone.

This is the only dignity left, the single
Death without purpose and without understanding

Like birds boys drop with catapults. Not comprehending
Denudes us of the personal aim and angle,
And so we are perfect sacrifice to nothing.

"GOODBYE THEN THE ISLAND COLONISED
BY IDEOGRAMS"

Goodbye then the island colonised by ideograms,
Of poverty and moongazing, hate and gardens,
Where the soul is shallower than a bowl of tea
And negative as water. And goodbye also
The opposite island of Gothic paradigms
Whom history too heavily burdens,—
Goodbye my white home in a lachrymose sea,
Too wise to be true, too stupid to be false.

Goodbye the stone angels and plush chairs,
The solicitor's plates worn to anonymity,
The parks where the duke's deer wander, the spring
A national resurrection, the lawyers, the liars:
Goodbye equally my kind and consanguinity,
Now all that is left is always everything.

SACRED ELEGIES

ELEGY I

I

From this window where the North Atlantic
Takes the crow in my mind home in a short line

Over the kissing fish in the wave, and the mine
Where the sailor clasps his death as mermaid like
Sex of a knife in the bed, from this window
Watching I see the farewelling seasons fall
Ever between us like rain. And the lachrymal
Memory, trailing its skirts, walks like a widow
Across those seas looking for home. O the Dido
Heart! Sail, sail the ships ever away from us all.

II

Then at this midnight as instant as the bell
That bangs the sailor from his bed to Europe,
I see tomorrow grow a tree of hope
Outside the window where, like a branch with a ball,
Your face of kisses hangs in my love
Shattered and happy. The sixteen winds that blow
The small seeds into each other's arms below,
The birds to their boughs above, the sad and evil
Everywhere, shall bring to you, if nothing else avail,
The love that, never coming, always goes.

III

To cross the divide and desert of this distance
Only a hand is enough. Like the seamew sweeping
The wave with a wing to rise up weeping
The parted heart shall with a bird's persistence
Cross seven oceans to its proper home. The pigeon
With a hundred hieroglyphics at its claw
Less laden drops down with what's waited for

Than the sea-weary home-comer returning. O let love
imagine
Meetings of the long parted at the door
Of expectation with smiles in the margin.

IV

Lovers for whom the world is always absent
Move in their lonely union like twin stars
Twining bright destinies around their cause:
They dazzle to shadow with a meridian present
The wallflower world. Redundant it shall resent
The kiss that annihilates and the gaze that razes.
O from their clasp a new astronomy rises
Where, morning and evening, the dominant Venus
Dismisses all sad worlds that turn between us,
And we shall kiss behind our mask of faces.

ELEGY II

I

Peace for explorers who come late upon water
I call the kiss of the foot on its native stone
After the separation of seas and the strange zone.
The madmen wandering across wildernesses, later
Look up and see the palatial womb and the home.
The maternal mirage lifts up its arms and says, 'Come'.
Cold under bridges a stranger freezes. The lost
Tankers heading their sad cortege in from the North

Not knowing which hemisphere gave them birth,
Shall sigh up their smoke sinking at last to rest.

II

Speak, then, of peace where the white child lies quiet
Sleeping in shadows between privation and pain:
Where the pink daughter drops back to bed again
After the visitor in the sheets, and red as riot
My father rises and condemns society.
Let me speak of peace among the proletariat
Protesting against life with a flag and a slogan,
Resigned to the empty gesture and the empty
Belly. Speak, then, of peace before death began
Foreclosing on the not yet buried man.

III

The Decalogue is written on their sheets
Where, watching life through windows, (the fish
Flying in wind, tattering trees with wishes,)
Exiled from existence, the invalids, like secrets,
Inhabit amber rooms. Only the dream completes
The landscape of that odd island where they dwell
With the two-headed child and the ghost. Their lives
File past the foot of the bed like negatives.
O the castaways in bedrooms! Exiled they shall
See Patmos visions exalting all that survives.

IV

Far from his home he dies in beds or deserts
With all the necessary angels at his head,
The lover in fever and poverty. The remembered
Image of Love comes down and, hushing his hurts,
Folds him in wide arms and takes him home to that dream
For which he is always seeking. The maternal
Mirage emerges in tremors of eternal
Concern. 'Come to the womb, come, for it is home.'
O invalids in love and indigence, return
To the hands of stars and the universal bosom!

"MY TALL DEAD WIVES"

My tall dead wives with knives in their breasts
Gaze at me, I am guilty, as they roll
      Like derelicts in my tempests,
Baring their innocence to the dirty pole
Whirled upon which I am a world at rest.

But restless in the bed of the will of things
I sleep with knives: the wave overhead
      Shall kiss with fangs
Red with the lipstick of their dead love
Above me as I lie in the grave of my bed.

O sex of crystal, foretell expiation
That like a feather, lightly, upon a father

Fall shall from the pain of the immolation:
      Then let me gather
Nothing but vipers to my satisfactions.

Like women of windows all red in morning
My wives walk down roads in rags and tears.
I know where they go and with what meaning.
      Everywhere is their
Wide and wilderness world beyond redeeming.

TO MY MOTHER

Most near, most dear, most loved and most far,
Under the window where I often found her
Sitting as huge as Asia, seismic with laughter,
Gin and chicken helpless in her Irish hand,
Irresistible as Rabelais, but most tender for
The lame dogs and hurt birds that surround her,—
She is a procession no one can follow after
But be like a little dog following a brass band.

She will not glance up at the bomber, or condescend
To drop her gin and scuttle to a cellar,
But lean on the mahogany table like a mountain
Whom only faith can move, and so I send
O all my faith and all my love to tell her
That she will move from mourning into morning.

TO ANY MEMBER OF MY GENERATION

What was it you remember?—the summer mornings
Down by the river at Richmond with a girl,

And as you kissed, clumsy in bathing costumes,
History guffawed in a rosebush. O what a warning—
If only we had known, if only we had known!
And when you looked in mirrors was this meaning
Plain as the pain in the centre of a pearl?
Horrible tomorrow in Teutonic postures
Making absurd the past we cannot disown?

Whenever we kissed we cocked the future's rifles
And from our wild-oat words, like dragon's teeth,
Death underfoot now arises: when we were gay
Dancing together in what we hoped was life,
Who was it in our arms but the whores of death
Whom we have found in our beds today, today?

DAVID GASCOYNE

IN DEFENCE OF HUMANISM

The face of the precipice is black with lovers;
The sun above them is a bag of nails; the spring's
First rivers hide among their hair.
Goliath plunges his hand into the poisoned well
And bows his head and feels my feet walk through his
                                  brain.
The children chasing butterflies turn round and see him
                                  there,
With his hand in the well and my body growing from his
                                  head.
And are afraid. They drop their nets and walk into the
                                wall like smoke.

The smooth plain with its rivers listens to the cliff
Like a basilisk eating flowers.
And the children, lost in the shadows of the catacombs,
Call to the mirrors for help:
'Strong-bow of salt, cutlass of memory,
Write on my map the name of every river.'

A flock of banners fight their way through the telescoped
                                  forest

And fly away like birds towards the sound of roasting
                                                    meat.
Sand falls into the boiling rivers through the telescopes'
                                                    mouths
And forms clear drops of acid with petals of whirling
                                                    flame.
Heraldic animals wade through the asphyxia of planets,
Butterflies burst from their skins and grow long tongues
                                                    like plants,
The plants play games with a suit of mail like a cloud.

Mirrors write Goliath's name upon my forehead,
While the children are killed in the smoke of the
                                                    catacombs
And lovers float down from the cliff like rain.

KYRIE

Is man's destructive lust insatiable? There is
Grief in the blow that shatters the innocent face.
Pain blots out clearer sense. And pleasure suffers
The trial thrust of death in even the bride's embrace.

The black catastrophe that can lay waste our worlds
May be unconsciously desired. Fear masks our face;
And tears as warm and cruelly wrung as blood
Are tumbling even in the mouth of our grimace.

How can our hope ring true? Fatality of guilt
And complicated anguish confounds time and place;

While from the tottering ancestral house an angry voice
Resounds in prophecy. Grant us extraordinary grace,

O spirit hidden in the dark in us and deep,
And bring to light the dream out of our sleep.

INFERNO

One evening like the years that shut us in,
Roofed by dark-blooded and convulsive cloud,
Led onward by the scarlet and black flag
Of anger and despondency, my self:
My searcher and destroyer: wandering
Through unnamed streets of a great nameless town,
As in a syncope, sudden, absolute,
Was shown the Void that undermines the world:
For all that eye can claim is impotent—
Sky, solid brick of buildings, masks of flesh—
Against the splintering of that screen which shields
Man's puny consciousness from hell: over the edge
Of a thin inch's fraction lie in wait for him

Bottomless depths of roaring emptiness.

LOWLAND

Heavy with rain and dense stagnating green
Of old trees guarding tombs these gardens
Sink in the dark and drown. The wet fields run

Together in the middle of the plain. And there are heard
Stampeding herds of horses and a cry,
More long and lamentable as the rains increase,
From out of the beyond.

                     O dionysian
Desire breaking that voice, released
By fear and torment, out of our lowland rear
A lofty, savage and enduring monument!

WINTER GARDEN

The season's anguish, crashing whirlwind, ice,
Have passed, and cleansed the trodden paths
That silent gardeners have strewn with ash.

The iron circles of the sky
Are worn away by tempest;
Yet in this garden there is no more strife:
The Winter's knife is buried in the earth.
Pure music is the cry that tears
The birdless branches in the wind.
No blossom is reborn. The blue
Stare of the pond is blind.

And no-one sees
A restless stranger through the morning stray
Across the sodden lawn, whose eyes
Are tired of weeping, in whose breast
A savage sun consumes its hidden day.

EVE

Profound the radiance issuing
From the all-inhaling mouth among
The blonde and stifling hair which falls
In heavy rivers from the high-crowned head,
While in the tension of her heat and light
The upward creeping blood whispers her name:
Insurgent, wounded and avenging one,
In whose black sex
Our ancient culpability like a pearl is set.

VENUS ANDROGYNE

With gaze impaired by heavy haze of sense
And sleep-dust, see: the blasphemy of flesh!
The breast is female, groin and fist are male
But the red sphinx is hidden underneath the
Weed-rank hair: muscle and grain
Of man inextricably twined
With woman's beauty.

Stand up, thorn
Of double anguish born, and pierce
The gentle athlete flank, that fierce pain
May merge like honey with the spirit's blood,
Purging desire: with agony atone
For such abhorrent heresy of seed,
And weld twin contradictions in a single fire!

ODEUR DE PENSEE

Thought has a subtle odour: which is not
Like that which hawthorn after rainfall has;
Nor is it sickly or astringent as
Are some scents which round human bodies float
Diluting sweat's thick auras. It's not like
Dust's immemorial smells, which lurk
Where spiders nest, in shadows under doors
Of rooms where centuries have died, and rest
In clouds along the blackening cracked floors
Of sties and closets, attics and wrecked tombs...
Thought's odour is so pale that in the air
Nostrils inhale, it disappears like fire
Put out by water. Drifting through the coils
Of the involved and sponge-like brain it frets
The fine-veined walls of secret mental cells,
Brushing their fragile fibre as with light
Nostalgic breezes: And it's then we sense
Remote presentiment of some intensely bright
Impending spiritual dawn, of which the pure
Immense illumination seems about to pour
In upon our existence from beyond
The edge of Knowing! But of that obscure
Deep presaging excitement shall remain
Briefly to linger in dry crannies of the brain
Not the least breath when fear-benumbed and frail
Our dying thought within the closely-sealed
Bone casket of the skull has flickered out,
And we've gone down into the odourless black soil.

FÊTE

After long thirst for sky, there was the sky,
That aether lake: vast azure canopy
Intensely stretched between horizons' ends!
Along the quays
The panes of opening windows flashed like wings,
Weaving long rays among the leafless trees;
Sirens of drifting barges sang:
And the whole day
Drank in the fecund flowing of the sky.

And on the outskirts of the town
Where the last house-blocks take their vacant stare
Across the straggling zone, and rusty streams
Among brown squares of threadbare soil
Persist their irrigating ooze, a savage train
Tore through a cutting with triumphant screams,
Releasing streamers of thick whirling breath
Which climbed and were suspended like presentiments on
                                                high . . .

Once more the earth, its buried spirit stirred,
Aspired towards the Summer's splendid bursting
And an illustrious death.

                                        Paris, 1938

SPRING MCMXL

London Bridge is falling down, Rome's burnt, and
                                            Babylon
The Great is now but dust; and still Spring must
Swing back through Time's continual arc to earth.
Though every land become as a black field
Dunged with the dead, drenched by the dying's blood,
Still must a punctual goddess waken and ascend
The rocky stairs, up into earth's chilled air,
And pass upon her mission through those carrion ranks,
Picking her way among a maze of broken brick
To quicken with her footsteps the short sooty grass
                                            between;
While now once more their futile matchwood empires
                                      flare and blaze
And through the smoke men gaze with bloodshot eyes
At the translucent apparition, clad in trembling nascent
                                            green,
Of one they can still recognise, though scarcely under-
                                            stand.

BIOGRAPHICAL NOTES

T. S. ELIOT (1888—), born in St. Louis, educated at Harvard, the Sorbonne, and Oxford; "Prufrock and Other Observations" 1917, "The Waste Land" 1922, "The Hollow Men" 1925, "Ash Wednesday" 1930, "Murder in the Cathedral" (verse play) 1935, "Four Quartets" 1944, and several books of essays.

EZRA POUND (1885—), born in Idaho, studied at Hamilton College, taught at the University of Pennsylvania 1905—1907; "A Lume Spento" 1908 (published in Venice), "Personæ" 1909, "Lustra" 1916, "Personæ: Collected Poems" 1926, "A Draft of XXX Cantos" 1933, "The Fifth Decad of Cantos" 1937, and many essays and translations.

EDITH SITWELL (1887—), with her brothers Osbert and Sacheverell edited "Wheels" 1916—1921, a calendar of modernist poetry; "Collected Poems" 1930, "Street Songs" 1942, "Green Song" 1944, "The Song of the Cold" 1945.

W. H. AUDEN (1907—), educated at Oxford; "Poems' 1930, "The Orators" 1932, "Look, Stranger!" 1936, "Another Time" 1940, "New Year Letter" 1941, "For the Time Being" 1945; plays in collaboration with Isherwood: "The Dog Beneath the Skin" 1935, "The Ascent of F6" 1936, "On the Frontier" 1938; visited Iceland, Spain, and China; emigrated to America 1939.

C. DAY LEWIS (1904—), educated at Oxford, schoolmaster; "Collected Poems 1929—1933", "A Time to Dance" 1935, "Overtures to Death" 1938, "Word Over All' 1943.

STEPHEN SPENDER (1909—), educated at Oxford; "Poems" 1933, "Trial of a Judge" (verse play) 1938, "The Still Centre" 1939, "Ruins and Visions" 1942.

LOUIS MACNEICE (1907—), educated at Oxford, lecturer in Greek; "Poems" 1933, "The Earth Compels" 1936, "Autumn Journal" 1939, "Plant and Phantom" 1941, "Springboard" 1944.

WILLIAM EMPSON (1907—), educated at Cambridge, professor of English literature in Japan and China; "Poems" 1935, "The Gathering Storm" 1940.

RONALD BOTTRALL (1906—), educated at Cambridge, lectured on English literature in Helsingfors, Singapore, Florence, British Council Representative in Stockholm and Rome; "The Loosening" 1931, "Festivals of Fire" 1935, "The Turning Path" 1939, "Farewell and Welcome" 1945.

DYLAN THOMAS (1914—), a leader of the Welsh literary movement; "18 Poems" 1934, "Twenty-five Poems" 1936, "The Map of Love" (verse and prose) 1939.

GEORGE BARKER (1913—); "Poems" 1935, "Calamiterror" 1937, "Lament and Triumph" 1941, "Eros in Dogma" 1944; like Auden has emigrated to America.

DAVID GASCOYNE (1916—), lived in France in the late thirties; "Poems 1937—1942".